OUR CRUISE THROUGH ASIA

A PICTORIAL REVIEW FROM AUSTRALIA TO JAPAN

CLAUDIA AND KEITH ZACHARIAS

AuthorHouse™
1663 Liberty Drive
Bloomington, IN 47403
www.authorhouse.com
Phone: 1-800-839-8640

First published by AuthorHouse 5/3/2010

ISBN: 978-1-4490-1882-5 (sc)

Library of Congress Control Number: 2009910250

Printed in the United States of America
Bloomington, Indiana

This book is printed on acid-free paper.

authorHOUSE®

CRUISING THE TIGER ECONOMIES

Indonesia - Singapore - Malaysia - Thailand
Vietnam - Hong Kong – Philippines – China – Korea – Alaska - Canada

Contents

Introduction

Groggily I woke enough to look at my watch from the light in the attendant's station next to my Business Class aisle seat; it was 3:00 am Los Angeles time. We had been flying for five hours of a 14 hour flight to Sydney, Australia where we would board a cruise ship for a 62 day tour of Asia. My wife, Claudia, in the window seat next to me was curled up in a ball under a blanket and in a deep sleep. I had to smile...there is something special for me about a female curled up with a blanket. Maybe it is my earliest memory of my mother holding my two brothers and me on her lap with blankets as we all took an afternoon nap in a rocking chair, or perhaps it is the memory of my young children similarly curled up with their mother. Whatever, it certainly has a warm spot in my heart and makes me wish I could curl up around her now, as I often do. In this instance though it makes me think of all the wonderful places we have been together; such places as the blazing hearth of our house in winter-time Santa Fe or a berth in a train winding around a mountain pass — but mostly just snuggling in our own wonderful bed at home, watching news shows or maybe a movie.

We love to travel together and are just thrilled to be on this trip now because, for the past two years, we have had very restricted travel because of health problems; first me and then her. We no long take our health and ability to travel for granted — it could be over within a heart-beat — or the lack of one.

"Would you like some orange juice?" a stewardess asked, displaying a tray filled with glasses of orange juice, apple juice and water.

I declined with a shake of my head and drifted back to my thoughts regarding our decision to go on this adventure. There is a certain amount of trepidation in deciding on a trip when it is for more than two months. This would be the first time we have ever been gone that long. The brochure advertising this trip had come in the mail, one of at least two a week of vacation offers, but this one caught my eye. I traveled for work as a certified computer and financial auditor for fifteen years in the Americas, Europe and even some in the Middle-East, but never in Asia. We kicked the idea around for some weeks, discussing all the pros and cons: Can we afford it? Can we be gone that long? Do we want to be gone that long? In the end it was decided by price...a call to the cruise line revealed they were offering deals at sixty percent of the normal price, perhaps because of the world-wide recession, we guessed. We were surprised; presently we both got on the phone with the cruise line and negotiated details and, liking what we heard, we put the reservation on hold for 24 hours. During that time we rolled the idea around; the deciding factor was that we had fared pretty well during the financial downturn of the past couple of years by putting most of our assets into U.S. Treasury bonds more than a year ago, so the negative financial impact to us was eased. Also, our health was reasonably good, for our age, which hasn't always been the case and won't always be again. After discussions between us, we decided to take the challenge and we confirmed our reservations — now we're on our way!

I always look at a venture like this as a series of milestones i.e. deciding on the trip, organizing the operations at home, packing, getting to the airport and eventually boarding the ship.

Our first leg of the journey was from Houston to Los Angeles where we stopped to see our youngest daughter, Betsy, who was in her second year of college. We spent four days with her before boarding this flight to Sydney, Australia. It is strange, for as much as you worry about children, for me the youngest being a daughter, was more worrisome than any of the other four, two boys and two girls.

That aside, my thoughts focused on things I might have forgotten. However our eldest son Andrew lives on our property and helps manage our apartments, so that any emergencies when we are gone can be handled by him.

The trip planning for Claudia was daunting, especially with some 30 formal nights on the ship. These are jacket and tie dress for dinner affairs where men wear tuxedos or suits while women dress mostly in long evening gowns. Also we were going to be in extreme climactic conditions, from the tropics to the cold of early spring Alaska. The information from the cruise line does give you some guidance in what kind of temperatures to expect but largely you are on your own. We packed a lot and had to pay enormous over-weight fees at check-in with the airline.

CHAPTER 1
SYDNEY, AUSTRALIA & BOARDING

Once in Sydney we were tired as we got off the plane but found our luggage, all 6 bags (big bags) and proceeded through customs. A nice lady from customs came over to Claudia and asked where we were from and said we could go through the express line and she put a sticker on each of our bags. We got on the other side of the customs line, rented a luggage cart to pile our bags on and walked toward the exit where we saw a lady holding up a Holland America sign; she confirmed we were on her roster, so we joined her group of about twenty couples and waited for more people.

During this time Claudia said she needed to go to the ladies room; the agent lady informed her it was just a little down the hall and she left. Five minutes passed and Claudia had not returned and the group I was standing with was starting to move towards the buses. Frantic, I asked a couple standing next to me to watch my bags while I went to look for her; I went into the area of the ladies room and no sign of her, I asked one of the security persons to check for her but they were too busy to do anything. I went back to the Holland America agent and she said, "Oh, don't worry, she will show up some place."

Fifteen minutes went by and still no Claudia; now the agent also became concerned and summoned two lady security people who got on their radios. A dozen security people started the search; one lady checked in the woman's restroom but she was not there. The search went on for at least another 15 minutes and the search area was being widened by the minute; then there was a crack on the radio. Someone found her in a parking lot. By now our group was nearly all loaded on the bus that would take us to the ship. One of the agents took Claudia back inside the terminal and finally the lost was found. Whew!

It was about 9:00 am when our buses pulled away from the airport and the driver announced he had been told to give us a city tour because the ship was not ready for boarding until 3:00 pm. We were all furious; we had been flying seventeen hours and we all wanted to have a shower and take a nap. No one was in the mood for a city tour but that's what we got and it turned out very well as these things sometimes do.

Sydney is a beautiful city, very clean and manicured, so in the next four hours we had been from one end to the other with lots of stops for restrooms and pictures; however, our camera was with the luggage. Finally we got to the ship terminal and much to our chagrin there were hundreds of people standing in front of the terminal building with their luggage, all waiting to get on the ship. The guards at the front gate were instructed not to let anyone past that point. We joined the block-long line snaking in front of the terminal building and finally three guys in a little enclosed moving truck came and gathered everyone's luggage. Personally, I had no confidence that we would ever see our luggage again but it did eventually show up at the door of our stateroom. Two hours went by before the doors were opened and people started being processed; then the paperwork took nearly another two hours. It was a long day, actually two days.

When Claudia and I got to the table to check in, the room number they had on their manifest was different from the one previously assigned to us. We had paid for an outside room on deck 3 which had a window but not one that opened. We had a similar stateroom on an earlier cruise and found it to be quite satisfactory. Comparing rooms on ships we have discovered that the premium rooms higher up on the ship are more affected by rough seas while the lower decks are considerably smoother. Before we had always stayed in rooms that had a balcony but on this trip we ordered too late and they were all gone. So when the lady behind the desk said, "No, your room number has been changed to 7066," I didn't say anything. I knew this was a premium room with a balcony and I felt sure they would realize the mistake sooner or later. But we quietly finished the check-in process. When we went to our room, to our pleasant surprise, it <u>was</u> a room with a balcony but even better just off our veranda was the Sydney Opera House. I can't remember if Claudia cried but it was a great moment. She had been to Sydney before, some thirty years ago, and had often raved about the beauty of this structure. Our room was larger then the one we had signed up for; it had a sofa that formed a small sitting room. We were thrilled, we have been upgraded before but not for free and not this big an upgrade. All the trauma of traveling and getting on the ship was soon forgotten.

We started to get acclimated to the room and soon our luggage showed up. We unloaded the suitcases into drawers and hanging closets; they filled up soon. To manage our clothing we had to put the cold weather clothes in suitcases which we could put under the bed.

We were going over the daily activity list when the announcement came over the loud speaker that it was time for the life boat drill; this, of course, is mandatory at the beginning of every cruise. The announcement told everyone to take one of the life preserver vests that are stored in the closet and then proceed to the life-boat station that is posted in big letters on the back of the cabin door. The elevators are not used during these drills except for the handicapped, so we all trundled down the stairs to the 3rd deck where the life boats are stored. Then the crew lines everybody up, men in back against the wall, women and children in the front. The gender make up of the passengers soon became apparent and a little shocking to me and the other men — there were more then two women for each man.

Maybe those are the numbers when we reach this age; many men are no longer with us and the women are left to live out their lives alone and take cruises, I guess. It reminds me of who we are on the ship; the Lucky Ones? We have had enough success to be able to afford this vacation and are healthy enough to be able to travel. The females are here as singles, widows or divorcees; the men just about all have a female partner. There are a few gay guys and maybe some lesbians, but the bulk of the unattached females are just traveling alone or with another single woman.

It made me wonder what went on in their lives — for the most part you never know. Our experience on other cruises taught us that we all accept each other at face value; there is little or no discussion of kids or other life events like divorces or deaths though most people will talk about their careers. Conversations are largely about other cruises; we all love to exchange cruise stories and the day's events.

Cruise ships traditionally have two sittings for dinner and everyone is expected to sign up for one or the other and on this cruise they had what they called "Open Seating". With this option you need to call the dining room each day and reserve a time and place. If you don't like either option or you miss your appointed time, there is a nice buffet available. Twice a week we have formal night which I discussed earlier. The other daily activities include breakfast and lunch whenever you want it; however, the evening meal is at 5:45 pm, or like us 8:00 pm.

It is difficult to explain all the things that go on during the day, to that end I copied an actual day's activities list that will hopefully give the reader an idea of the possible activities that are scheduled to occupy the guests.

The daily ship schedule

7:00 am, Fitness class

8:00   Mass is celebrated

8:30   Interdenominational devotion

9:00   Daily quiz and Sudoku, gold chain sales by the inch, Fitness class

9:30   Good morning with cruise director and First Officer, Olympic basketball

10:00 Horse Racing, big money bingo, social bridge, cooking class

11:00 Cruise speaker about Asia, cooking Asian food, spa class, art gallery class

12:30 pm, Line dance lessons

1:00   Spa 5 minute makeover, casino tournament, cooking desserts, trivia challenge

2:00   Shore excursions talk, social bridge meet

2:30   Cooking class breads, jewelry fashion show, sidewalk art sale

3:00   Sports activities, topaz show, high tea, ship officer tells about the ship

3:30   Drink mixing class, bingo

4:00   Wine tasting, evening prayer meet

5:00   Happy hour in various bars

5:45   First seating dinner, piano bar singing with Randall Powell our talented entertainer

8:00   Second seating dinner, first Showtime with the ship's singers and dancers

9:00   DJ in Crows Nest bar, coffee, cognac and classical music with strings 5th level bar

10:00 Second show time, dancing in three of the four bars

11:00 Midnight snack bar, DJ and the ship's orchestra plays in Crows Nest bar.

The other activities on board include swimming, gambling, reading and walking around the ship. For those who are disciplined, there is a full gym. The cruise director is also charged with holding all sorts of special events. There are sales to lure the passengers into buying costume jewelry, high-end jewelry, gold chains sold by the inch and clothing appropriate to each travel destination. They have all kinds of things you didn't know you needed and it is all "On Sale" at 40% off and Duty Free.

Each day we had lectures by two men, one on the history of the areas we were about to visit and the other described upcoming shore excursions. The historian was a linguist of some repute, a retired professor from the University of Vancouver in Canada…his lectures were not to miss. He was a superb speaker with an interesting and unique analysis of human behavior from the perspective of the languages. He postulated that language establishes a commonality in terms of beliefs and motivations. It ties you to other peoples, as in who you are most likely to go to war with or against, whom you will ally with, etc. He has lived and taught in various countries around Asia; he explained and demonstrated with slides, the history of the languages in the areas and the impact it has had on those who allied and/or warred with each other. These events created the societies we were going to be visiting. I have to give the cruise line credit; they had a real winner with this lecturer.

The other guy was from Peru and speaks quite broken English, in spite of the considerable time he has been doing this. He explained the upcoming shore excursions so people can decide which they are interested in and which ones they can manage, as many of us have physical limitations. He makes some real faux pas from time to time, his latest, "smelling the incest" instead of "smelling the incense." His bloopers have become dinner table jokes and apparently no one has the heart to correct him. The ladies at our table have decided it will be hard to hear either word from now on without chuckling.

One of the interesting things about cruise ships we have noticed over the years is the public announcement system. When the Captain speaks, it is piped into the public areas and the rooms so all can hear; however, when the Cruise Director speaks about all the other activities, many vitally important, it is not piped into the rooms. So the quickest way to hear the announcements is to run and crack open the door to the hallway and listen. The Cruise Director calls us gophers; we as they just stick our heads out of our holes. It was amusing in one instance where Claudia ran to the door in her underwear and opened the door just enough to hear while hiding behind it. I noticed the woman across the hall also in her underwear with her door open enough to hear and trying to hide herself behind it. When I was in college I had a professor who liked to use an axiom that it seems apropos to this situation.

"If a man from Mars came down and observed this situation, given mankind had developed the technology to put a man on the moon and return him safely back to the earth 40 years ago, he surely should be able to devise a better message delivery system than this for cruise ship staterooms!"

Sidney opera house

us and opera house

Chapter 2

Why do we cruise?

At the end of each segment of this sixty day cruise, about every two weeks, some people get off and others come aboard. In our two months we have had five changes in passengers. Only about three hundred of us, out of the total of fourteen hundred, are on all the way from Sydney to Vancouver. At the end of each segment, the company sends out to all of us a questionnaire about how we rate things on the ship, from food to cabin service.

I don't fill those things out but Claudia does for us. She would lie on the bed and read the questions and ask my input. In the questionnaire, one item caught my attention; they asked, "Why did you select this cruise?"

1. Do you want to get away from it all and relax?

2. Do you go for the food?

3. Do you go to see the places and go on land excursions?

4. Do you just want to be on the ship for the life style?

5. Do you go for the speakers on board?

These posed a real thought process for us; why indeed do we cruise?

1. One thing we can settle on for sure was that once you get on board you never have to handle luggage again until the end of the trip.

2. This allows us to go see places without going to airports and struggling with luggage.

3. We like the isolation from news and the humdrum of life at home.

4. We like to read and I write, as with this little remembrance.

5. We dress for dinner or not. We like to converse with tablemates.

6. There is nightly entertainment and lots of daytime activities.

7. They have interesting speakers that relate to the history, geography and other facts about the places you are about to visit.

8. They have someone to explain each of the land excursions coming up at the next port of call and the points of interest and the pitfalls of each.

There are also many personal reasons why cruises appeal to many of us at this time in our lives.

1. People you have known throughout your life sometimes drift away.

2. People move from their home area to be near children as they age.

3. They get a divorce or experience the death of a spouse which leaves the remaining partner an odd person out in a group of couples.

4. People retiring often move for climate considerations and miss old friends.

5. This leaves large groups of people that are ripe for a temporary relationship with other couples on a cruise ship.

6. Relationships can develop into lasting friendships for those who keep up with each other and sometimes even travel together in the future.

7. Cruising is a controlled safe way to see new places.

8. The ship offers assistance in arranging shore excursions and keeps track of everyone on such excursions.

9. The cruise ship is a place to go where everything is done for you, there is no cooking, making beds or doing laundry and if you choose you can send your laundry out to be done. All you need to do is sleep, read, eat and of course, sightsee if you choose.

10. The bottom line situation is that cruise ships fill this need or desire of people to move about on a 'Hole in the water into which lots of people pour money;' the daffynition of a boat.

11. It is a social life with new people who don't know your past and you don't know theirs.

CHAPTER 3
THE GREAT BARRIER REEF

Our first shore excursion was at the Whitsunday Island chain in the Coral Sea just off the east side of Australia. In ports where there are no docking facilities for big ships, small boats, "tenders," usually the ship's life boats, are used to transport people to the shore. From there tourists join whichever tour they plan to go on. We signed up to see the Great Barrier Reef and for us a large catamaran boat that was going to take us 30 miles to the reef came directly to the ship, this meant we didn't have to take one of the tenders to the shore.

The Great Barrier Reef is a formation created from the coral that grows there. Coral is a living organism that attaches itself to shallow submerged rocks and land formations that exist in this area. The Great Barrier Reef is several thousand miles long and the width varies from a few thousand meters to several kilometers along its length. The reef is a land formation which was dry land until some 10 million years ago when it became submerged because the ocean levels rose as the glaciers from the preceding ice age melted. Living coral is a phenomenon that occurs on land submerged in warm shallow tropical waters or on any solid structure such as sunken ships.

As usual, we and the others that signed up for land tours proceeded to the auditorium where we were given a sticker with a number on it; we would then be called by groups and instructed to go to the lower deck to the gangplank. In this case we boarded a catamaran that held more then 300 people. Soon we were headed out some 30 miles to reach a permanent floating platform where people could snorkel, scuba dive or just view the world of the reef. We didn't wish to get wet, so we entered down into the submerged glass area of the platform where we could view the fish and coral immediately under the platform. The water was murky from a hurricane that had passed over the area a week before we got there.

Also, there was a submarine that held 50 people which toured around the area for 20 minutes; we all had to stand in line to get a turn in the sub. Once we crawled down into this narrow machine, we saw it had a single row of seats on each side that folded up against the windowed walls. Once at our seat, we flipped down the seats and sat looking out into the waters about twenty feet below the surface. The sub navigated within inches of the rock formations and all the various forms of coral imaginable. Staring directly at, or in some cases looking up at, these formations was incredible even though the water was murky from being stirred up by the hurricane just days earlier; the scene was still awesome.

The trip out to the platform was about 30 miles, 10 miles of which was in open seas. This meant there was no shelter from either the land mass of Australia or from the reef; either of which afforded the ability to stop or slow the effect of the open waters of the Pacific Ocean. The sea in this open water was rough; sailors would call this "8 to 10 foot seas." This means that the swells were up to 10 feet high which makes for a pretty rough ride in any craft, but in a catamaran it is worse because of the wide stance which catches the waves and pitches the boat unmercifully. About a quarter of the people got sea sick, including Claudia. We all thought it was bad going out…the trip back was far worse.

Claudia considered this excursion nearly worthless because of the murky water. She had seen the reef before on a previous trip and was awe struck at its beauty then. Well maybe that's a reason to come back and visit Australia at a later time.

Great Barrier Reef platform

CHAPTER 4

Cairns, Australia and the Tropical Rain Forest

We were docked when we awoke today at the harbor at Cairns, Australia. We signed up for a tour of a Rain Forest which we didn't even realize existed in Australia. We went to the auditorium where each of us got our numbered colored stickers which made us wards of the tour-guide for the day. It is the tour-guide's responsibility to counts heads each time everyone gets back on the bus to go to the next location. Everyone is responsible to get back at the exact time announced or suffer the ridicule of the rest of the passengers, if late.

We went by bus, "coach," in this part of the world, to a train that wound its way up a mountain in this Rain Forest some 20 miles from the port and up to about 1200 feet in elevation. The steam engine was old and the cars had no air conditioning; however, the temperature was not bad. We crawled up the mountain across huge gorges with spectacular waterfalls and through a dozen hand chiseled tunnels. The switchbacks were interesting as we could see the end of the train tagging along as we precariously traversed track that barely clung to the edge of the cliffs. A recorded broadcast in the cars told the story of the great grandfathers who toiled here and some that gave their lives in the construction of this railroad.

Half-way up it was announced that during WWII the allies had built the largest field hospital in the southern hemisphere on a flat plain we observed off to the right of the train. One can only imagine, or maybe we can't, envision the pain and suffering both physical and mental, that such a place witnessed. The horror that young men, just boys actually, went through experiencing the loss of limbs, eye sight and their general health. Malaria, of course, was a major cause of casualties in this part of the world then and still is now.

Once at the top there was a community consisting of tourist traps and restaurants. The one we visited had a deck built out over a ravine, jutting into the rainforest. It was shady and pleasantly cool and charming with the sounds of the jungle birds calling in the distance. We didn't have much time, an hour, before we had to be back at the bus so we quickly ate and managed to stop at a pharmacy to buy needed insect repellent.

The next stop was an aerial tram that would take us back down the mountain. It looked relatively new; when I asked an attendant at one of the stations he told us that it was built in the 90's. Riding over the Rain Forest in these six-person enclosed cars with air vents and open windows was an incredible experience. The thing that immediately struck me was the height of the trees. The top of the forest canopy, which I had estimated and later established, was two-hundred-fifty-feet tall. Looking at this jungle from the top down is an incredible experience, a scene not widely available, which is a shame. The jungle floor foliage is too thick to see through and it made me think of the stories where adventurers or armies, that for one reason or another, hacked their way through jungles. Riding over this mass of trees, brush and tangled vines made such a task look impossible.

Unfortunately at the bottom of the mountain and the end of our tram ride, the trip back to the ship tainted our memory of the event. Both the bus driver and the tour-guide miscounted our gaggle and when we were nearly back to the ship, the tour-guide got a call on her cell phone informing her that two people were still at the tram station. So rather than have the two take a cab, she decided we should turn around and go way back. The bus was crowded and uncomfortable and we were all furious and took the tour-guide to task. I confess that sitting in the seat behind the tour-guide I pointed out to her where she had gone wrong. The problem was that of organization. The trip down from the mountain peak involved stopping at three places to sightsee and one place where we switched to a different tram for the last-half of the journey. The guide at the top never specified any time when we all needed to be at the bottom. It was preposterous to assume that 42 people would all get to the bottom at the relatively the same time and we didn't. I asked her why they didn't have the two people take a cab and the tour company pay for it. She said they didn't think of that; I left it that there were simpler ways to handle such problems. She said she would fill out a report.

Cairns rainforest

CHAPTER 5

DARWIN AUSTRALIA

Darwin turned out disappointingly, to be a long bus ride. We did not go into the city which might have been more interesting but it was Sunday and everything was closed according to those we asked, including our Australian table-mates. Apparently the retail stores do not open on Sunday; much of rural America is still that way. The large city stores especially the big Wal-Mart types are open to allow weekend shopping. Traditionally, women were housewives and had the full week to shop for the family needs but now with most women in the work-force, this shopping is compressed into the weekend.

The first stop on our bus ride was the most entertaining. We visited a crocodile experimental station and breeding farm. They had a half-aborigine guy, thin and wiry, who teased the crocs into jumping out of the water after a piece of chicken he dangled from a cable apparatus with a pulley on each end like a clothes line. He would roll the chicken just above the crocs' heads and make them jump after it, which they did eagerly. The farm consisted of a dozen or so breeding pairs, each with their own pen, which was about 30 feet long and 15 feet wide with a water hole in the middle that sloped out at each side. He would toss chicken at them to make them move; he explained crocs are not able to see very well but can smell and hear extremely well.

We saw our first kangaroo at this farm in addition to some big birds similar to an ostrich.

We left the crocs to drive for an hour to Litchfield National Park, a huge plot of land 1500 sq km. Here the land drops several hundred feet at one place and because March is the end of the rainy season in Australia, there were two waterfalls that were active. There were also termite mounds that were more than 20 feet tall and 15 feet around, so we stopped and investigated these structures. Then we had lunch at a typical outback oasis, a bar that served some food and had the necessities of life for those who live out here and don't get to town often. The ride was long and there just wasn't much to see except it gave one an excellent feel for the vastness of the area which is where large cattle farms are the industry.

One interesting thing we observed was what they call "truck trains." These consist of a large truck tractor that pulls several trailers behind it, so instead of an 18 wheeler these are 72 wheelers or some number of wheels depending on the number of trailers. We saw these moving cattle, oil and gravel.

Darwin alligator farm

Darwin termite mound

CHAPTER 6

Komodo, Indonesia and the Dragons

Komodo is a remote island in a chain of islands in southern Indochina. We had the ship tenders, (life boats), take us ashore where we tromped half a mile to see four large Komodo Dragons, the world's largest lizards. They live wild on the island, so tourists are confined to groups of 25, guarded by several locals with forked canes about 8 feet long. Apparently this can be used to ward off any attacking dragons as they are man-eaters; the guide told us that of the 1500 people on the island nearly once a year a person usually a child gets eaten by the dragons. Some five tender loads from the ship, each holds 100+ people, descended on the tiny island all tromping through the forest to get a look at the Komodo Dragons…Claudia and I were among them. We were not sure about the actual danger to tourists, but it makes a good yarn and helps with collecting bigger tips at the end of the tour.

Because we didn't want to walk the entire two mile path, we were assigned one local young man, Poncho, to escort us back after we saw the dragons. Walking is a problem for me because I live with the results of a childhood disease called Legge Perthes that I contracted at age four. The orthopedists who know about it, say it is a condition that affects one in ten million male children or something like that. When I contracted the disease in the summer of 1947 at the height of the polio epidemic, the doctors thought that I had polio. Most of the events of that early childhood year are very vague except for one thing—the terror on my mother's face—I can see it yet. Of course I was too young to comprehend the implications of the situation and I don't think one can fully understand the feeling of one's parents in such a situation until you have children of your own.

The diseased hips caused me to have one short leg which put a strain on my lower back that turned arthritic by middle age; my hips are now both artificial. I have had two surgeries on my spine to scrape out the arthritis that was pinching off my spinal cord and paralyzing my legs.

Back to the Komodo Island, our guide Poncho, told us all about the island and took us to the shopping area and introduced us to his family. They were selling mementoes in a rickety stand, just a tin roof built on crooked poles; it was a sight. There was little time to shop; the vendors, as in most such places, are three deep hounding you to buy their stuff. We did buy some dragon figurines and two t-shirts.

The island itself was a green tropical beauty with low mountains and jungle greenery. The people we saw were poor beyond most American's comprehension; yet they seemed to have a cheery disposition. Poncho told us he was married and had a little boy, he ran out to greet us on our way back to the harbor. He was about three years old and was under the care of his paternal grandfather who looked as proud as any of us with a child of a child.

Komodo dragon

CHAPTER 7

BALI, INDONESIA

The only thing I knew about Bali before visiting there was the song and the scenes about "Bali Hai" from the musical South Pacific, a Rogers and Hammerstein production. Home to millions now, the tour-guide mentioned the Japanese occupation during the war. He was too young for first hand remembrance, so he was repeating what he had heard from his elders, which was horrific. The oppression and impressment memories had carried over into the second generation. We loaded onto a bus and drove and drove, stopping at a theater where we watched a one hour performance of a traditional show. It was the battle of Good against Evil although even with a document explaining the show; it was hard to determine which was which. They had a definite sense of humor especially in a scene where a dead monkey had a hard penis sticking up, which in the end turned out to be his tail, but the exploits with this were quite amusing. The garb of the actors was incredible. The fabric they have on this island was the admiration of all the women on the trip; most of us bought the four foot square pieces they were selling at every stop. The vendors were worse than the peskiest flies you have ever encountered; they come right in your face and beg you to buy their items. If you happen to buy from someone else, the first ones are crushed that you didn't buy from them. They use young kids especially pathetic looking young girls to do much of the begging. It is heart-breaking to watch their faces if you reject them; no doubt their elders know what works. I gave one such particularly emaciated girl two dollars, just as a matter of conscience; then her mother insisted I pay two more dollars for the packet of pictures she was selling and insisted I buy the packet. I just walked away. Then both the little girl and her mother thanked me by saying something I didn't understand and bowing to me. I did a quick bow in return and hustled to the bus to get away from this pack of beggars. The tour-guide saw my ordeal and said I had done a good thing, because if you buy the pack of pictures they probably only get a few pennies, but they can keep the money I gave them without having to account for their inventory to a "boss."

Next stop was a Hindu Temple where anyone wearing shorts or short skirts was required to wrap a piece of fabric around their waist and secure it with a yellow strip of fabric that served as a belt. The temple was beautifully decorated in magnificent colors and was an active temple. The guide explained the ceremony that was going on as a graduation of monks.

Next we proceeded up a mountain to have lunch at a restaurant overlooking a lake and the valley below. From there we went to the Bali National Museum of Art where the different stages of art development over the eons were displayed. The traditional art was fascinating. It was loaded with tiny figures of people and their various gods and goddesses but the most interesting to me was the harvesting of rice, lots of those. Nearly all showed the people working in the fields naked from the waist up, male or female. So I asked one of the museum officials about that and he told me before 1960 that was the way the women dressed working in the fields but after that time the females covered their breasts. Numerous other paintings showed how they harvested the rice. They cut the ripe rice and tied a bunch together with twine and carried these bundles off the fields to hang upside down out of the rain until it dried. When it was ready to be thrashed several methods were used according to the guy. They pound the rice stocks with the rice heads on a floor until all the kernels are out of the husk, or they have animals walk over the rice stalks, and sometimes they pound the heads with a thrashing stick. This consists of a bamboo stick with one end slit into thin strips which spread out and beat the rice kernels out of the husk. This is where we get the name "thrashing stick" as I think about it.

We next visited a wood-working shop that was truly incredible. The objects they carve from wood are mind-bogglingly, indescribable. Only the pictures associated with this story can begin to demonstrate what I am saying; however, because they are not three dimensional they do not show the full beauty. We watched workers, mainly women, working on crafting the fine, intricate work, while men were chopping huge tree-parts into manageable sizes — which could range from several feet long to only inches. We discussed this woodworking with our room steward before we left the ship and he told us that the Balinese are the experts in this craft and that other areas of Asia only make bad copies. We certainly didn't see anything comparable anywhere else.

The drive through the countryside was educational and beautiful. The rice paddies had men out working in them, pulling weeds to keep the fields clean of anything but the rice plants. One man and probably a son were spreading fertilizer on the newly planted rich shoots. I saw a man plowing with a team of buffalo in standing water. Having grown up on a dry land farm, I somehow assumed they would plow the land when it is dry but that was not the case here.

One item all of us on the bus were puzzled about was the presence small elegant shrines in the back yards of some of the more expensive looking homes. These, we found out, are used for storing ashes of ancestors and as a place for offerings.

Bali dancing girls

Bali wood carving

CHAPTER 8

SEMARANG, INDONESIA

Indonesia's fifth largest city is located on the North coast of the island of Java; it is an industrial city that dates back to the 9th century. By the end of the 15th century an Arab Islamic mullah established a boarding school here; in the 1920's Semarang it became known as the "Red City" when it became the center of the Communist Party on Java. The Japanese military occupied the city along with the rest of Java in 1942, during World War II. After Indonesian independence in 1945, Semarang became the capital of the Central Java Province.

We got off the ship at 6:30 am for a tour of the area which included a visit to the largest Buddhist monument in the world, the Borobudur Temple. Built between 750 and 850 AD it is considered one of the Seven Wonders of the World. The associated pictures show how massive it is. It took 120 years to build. The Great Pyramid in Egypt only took about 20 years and although they have a similar foot print this one is not as tall. The intricate decorative work helps explain the time difference for construction.

This temple was 130 km away from our port of entry and because of the narrow, crowded streets, we were only able to get to our destination and back to the ship by 4:00 pm, our scheduled sail-away time, by having a police escort. The police commandeered the oncoming traffic lane. The ride was a hoot, men were laughing and women were screaming as the four of our buses charged along on the wrong side of the road with cars and trucks honking and swerving out of the way. The whole excursion was a series of near misses and crazier than any amusement park ride.

Java is a beautiful place with rice paddies throughout the island, punctuated by farmer's shacks and bordered with palm trees in some areas. The place seemed teeming with life and, as in Bali, the roadside markets display the local fruits and vegetables. Going to our destination half way we switched from the bus to an 1800's train with two rickety small cars and a little antique engine the women dubbed, "The Little Engine That Could." The engine huffed and puffed and had to stop several times to allow the steam boiler to build up a head of steam so we could progress a few hundred yards at a time.

The most notable problem with the trip was the lack of toilet facilities anywhere along this route. When you are dealing with oldsters you need good facilities and they didn't have anything near that. At each of the two stops we waited for more than half an hour for the women's line to finish.

Once at the temple we walked around the massive exterior; it is approximately one football field long on each side and rises to a height of more than two hundred feet. Claudia and I, as most of those on the trip, didn't climb to the top for the "Great View", as announced by our guide, but the structure was spectacular in its detail. It is an Asian pyramid decorated with figures and designs of amazing intricacy from bottom to top. It is truly one of the wonders of the world and to boot one we had never even heard of.

We walked around to the opposite side of the temple and down a huge number of stairs to a restaurant where we had lunch under a network of shade tents set up for this purpose. This being in the tropics and at high noon gave the term 'hot lunch' new meaning. Drenching wet with our own sweat we all ate and got back on the buses via a string of the local pesky vendors and headed for the ship. We made a quick stop at a coffee factory that set out samples of coffee and tea with some small sweets; of course, there were a few dozen pesky vendors.

The road back to the ship was now a race as we were more then an hour late and the police and the bus drivers took even crazier chances than before.

Indonesia harbor

Indonesia rice fields

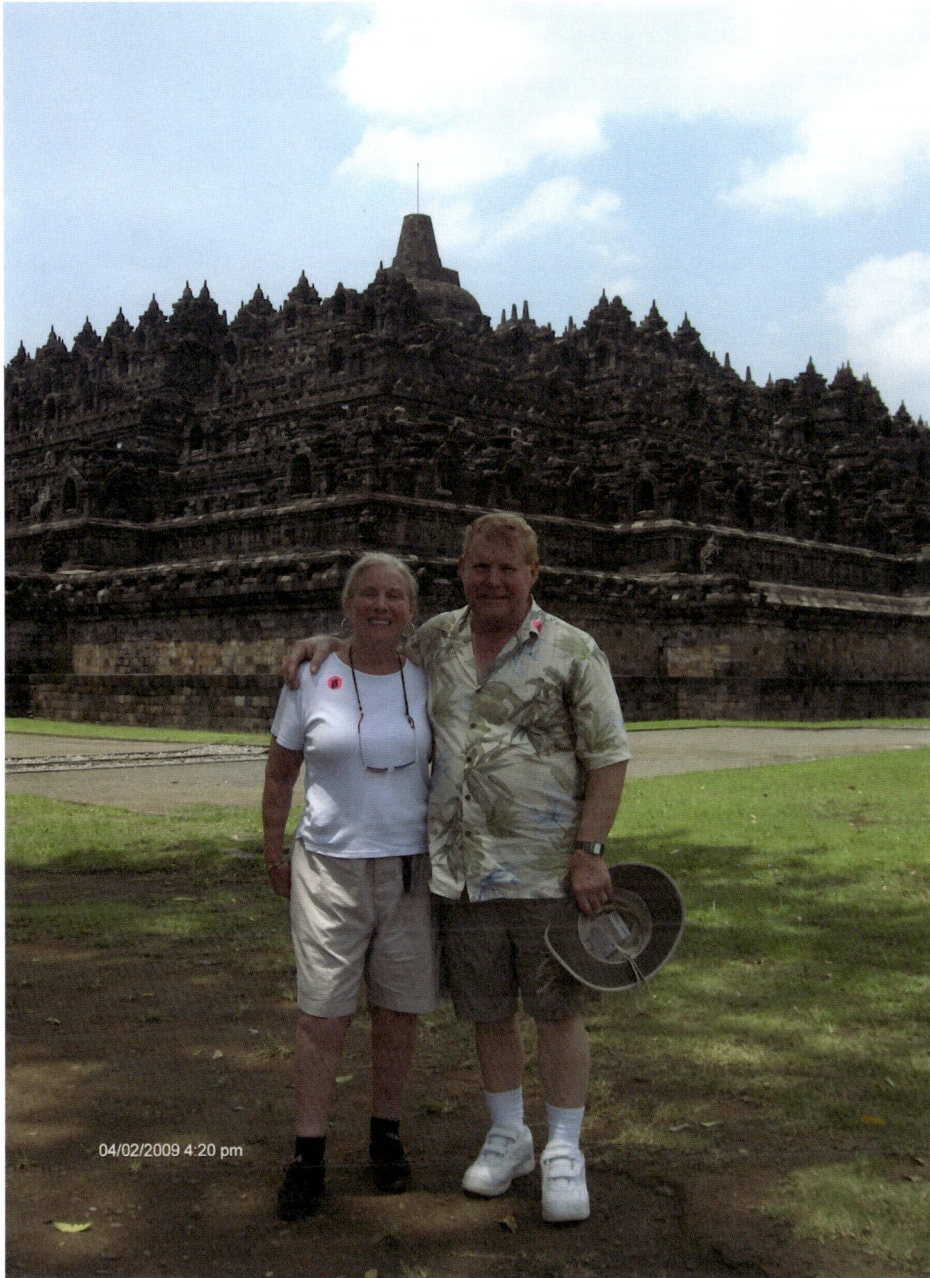

04/02/2009 4:20 pm

us & Borobudor Temple

CHAPTER 9

CROSSING THE EQUATOR

Initiation ceremonies for ship's crew members who have not crossed the equator before are a seafaring tradition. For cruise ships this ceremony is quite civil, not so for military or merchant marine ships. The ceremony on our ship started with a great decorated procession of the court of King Neptune, the Greek god of the water deities. He called Court to meet beside the decorated swimming pool. He sat on an over-decorated throne with several beautiful, female, bikini clad assistants whose job it was to lead in the struggling victims/initiates. King Neptune was the ship's piano man, a good natured extremely large man with a great wit; he is a fellow Texan with whom we became friends. We, along with many others, sat at his piano bar nightly and enjoyed a drink and joined the others waiting to go to dinner in a sing-a-long. He played this King Neptune role with great exuberance. Then with pomposity and fervor the newcomers' "pollywogs," were accused of dreamed up ridiculous offenses like "not puffing the guests pillows three time when they made the beds" or "not making drinks fast enough" in the case of the piano bartenderess whom he clowned around with every night. Once convicted, the pollywogs were rolled around on a table of flour and blue food-coloring and then dunked into the pool. It was all done with great merriment; everyone hoisted drinks and shouted slogans of 'dunk them' and 'guilty' until all were dunked.

The ceremony was fun but this was the equator and the sun was brutally hot around the pool so it was all done quickly. A ceremony like this had to be done in early afternoon because this was the slack time for the crew. Some of the older people, older than us (and we are all old), said that the cruise ships used to have a ceremony for the passengers as well as crew; it was a more civil exercise than for the crew but nevertheless all were initiated.

ships piano player from Texas

CHAPTER 10

SINGAPORE

At this stop, many of the people that had gotten on in Sydney or earlier ports disembarked. On a ship you embark when you get on and disembark when you get off. Last night was the last night we spent with the four Australian ladies we had shared our dinner-table with. They were sweet and particularly interesting as they told us all about Australia; we learned more from them than any other source.

We docked early morning, 6:00am, and the people disembarking made their way off by noon and those joining our cruise, embarking, started to come on about noon too. Those of us that just went shopping could slip off the ship at will and do what you do in Singapore…**shop**. We grabbed a cab and drove around to investigate the city; the cab driver was quite a good tour-guide and dropped us off at the two streets noted for fancy shops. This is a place for very rich people to shop, so we window shopped and then later went back to the mall close to the ship and got some things we needed.

Singapore is noted for its strict laws, spitting on the sidewalk is a $500 fine, etc. The city is beautiful, very well decorated with plants, palm trees and grass along all the roads and streets; everything is clean, clean, clean.

We only went to one historically important site, the Long Bar at the Raffles Hotel. The hotel was started, supposedly, by the first white guy to settle Singapore. We ordered the classic drink, a Singapore Sling; it was a little sweet but drinkable. While we were there the four Australian ladies, our table mates from the ship, came walking in. They left the ship, took their luggage to the airport and started a tour of the city. Their running into us was quite a coincidence; we all laughed about it, it was nice meeting them so unexpectedly.

We again bade them farewell with little hugs and well wishes on our respective travels. Watching them walk out the door, I thought about the fact that it was a fluke that they came in the same place at the same time we happened to be there. It was obvious we would probably never see them again. They were in and out of our lives just as so many other people are that you meet throughout your life.

So who does stay in your life? According to the "**Book of Zac**" it goes something like the following:

Well, your birth family, if you are lucky. You don't select them; you just arrive in a totally dependent and helpless state as a result of your parent's passion and with more than a little pain and anguish on behalf of your mother giving you life. In spite of that she kisses you a lot, feeds you and changes your dirty diapers. Your parents are proud of you when you take your first step and the first day you go to school — your mom cries and kisses you. They support you in all the things you "need" and try to guide you into being a proper adult, namely like them, and are usually horrified with your generational norms. All of this goes on for close to twenty years, at which point your parents are very glad when you become independent and move out. They still profess to love you…mostly with an eye on their old age at which time they hope you will feed them and change their diaper and so on.

In the growing up process you make friends who become close, at least for a while, and even some are "Best Friends Forever." It is my observation that this is truer for women than men. But the next big-time permanent person in your life is usually a spouse. They are attained by some combination of raging hormones and various trysts in cars parked in dark lonely places, which have been known to cause…expectations? Then the two of you spend your lives struggling to make a living, raise your family and hopefully plan for your retirement or some dysfunctional or functional version of that. Maybe go on a cruise and write a book about it, or as our grand-kids say, "Whatever".

In Singapore we shopped a while longer and got back on the ship just before sailing out of the harbor. This is the busiest of any port according to the announcement from "The Bridge" (the front of the ship where the captain and officers responsible for steering the ship work). I have never seen so many ships and boats of any and all descriptions moving around and anchored, doing whatever they do. The port is involved in the oil business; we passed a huge refinery facility and I noticed that we took on fuel while we were docked here. I assume that is one reason for many of the ships being here, because there are not that many refineries in this area of the world.

The city shops we visited were filled with young people shopping on this Saturday. Young couples with kids from a few months old to teenagers were bustling about and it was enjoyable to watch, after being on the ship where the average age is a few years from pushing up daisies. The city was very busy and there was no sign of a depression here. They seem to be doing well; it was nice to see so many nuclear families out shopping. I observed one mother struggling with her brood of three as she was trying clothes on them; a boy about six or seven was especially challenging.

I remember when my three brothers and I had to go shopping for "school clothes" with Mom; we hated it and were not very cooperative I'm afraid. We grew up on a farm and our only interest in going to town was the dime-store where they sold comic books and then stopping at the A&W Drive-In on the way home for a hamburger, French fries and root beer.

The population of Singapore looked basically Chinese, which corresponds with what we were told by those on the ship; everyone was courteous and extremely well mannered. I missed one photo op where a mother in her early thirties who was carrying a baby with a two year old daughter trailing along. Standing and with one hand the mother slipped a shoe on her foot then with neither saying anything the two year old squatted down to pull up the strap that went around mommies ankle. I couldn't get my camera out fast enough to capture the moment and once the mother saw me observing them, she smiled shyly. When I motioned for her to restage the event but she took the little girl and moved on. It made me feel bad like some how I violated her space or privacy.

We spent the next few days at sea and in our cabin planning our visits to the upcoming cities; which did not go well. Some tours were full and many we had no interest in. Eventually the director did get us on the excursions we wanted. If a tour is full they put people on standby. Because of health problems many people don't show up for tours at the last moment; we have done that ourselves.

Some passengers strike out on their own but we are more inclined to stick with organized tours because many places are hard to find and when you don't speak the language you can get frustrated at best or very lost at worst. Also we are not able to walk very far so if you can't find a taxi you can get marooned. There is a lot of security in being with a group organized by the ship. You won't get lost and if you are late the ship will wait for a group; whereas, with an individual they just leave you and you have to find your own way to the ship's next port of call.

CHAPTER 11

BANGKOK, THAILAND

The visit into Bangkok was a two day trip with an overnight stay at the Royal Orchid Sheraton Hotel — which is a beautiful place to stay. The sightseeing tour was a splendid trip on the river and the waterway canals. The city is called the Venice of Southeast Asia and the four hour boat trip, which moved around the city canal system, was a view into the heart of a culture. People live on the river, using it for washing, drinking and dumping their sewage in much the same way they do in Venice. They depend on the tides to move out the old contaminated water and replace it with fresh water from the Chao Phraya River. The city is close to its mouth and empties into the bay of Thailand and I was shocked to find out the area has twenty foot tides, some of the highest on earth, I was told.

The first thing that intrigued me about the twenty to thirty person taxi-boats we rode on was their power system. They use car engines with straight transmissions that sit on top and on back of the boat. They have a long shaft with a propeller on the end and they put it down in the water and go like crazy. They have eliminated the need for a shaft to go through the back of the boat eliminating the problem of leaking seals. The engines have a small radiator but water is pumped from the river through it to cool the engine. The driver sits in the back, by the engine, and lowers the shaft into the water and moving the shaft one way or the other is what turns the boat.

The people have the custom of not only bowing for everything, but these people put their hands together, palm to palm, fingers pointed upward in a prayer mode while they bow. They are very gracious and extremely friendly, a genuine pleasure to be around.

Our trip to Thailand was for me a most pleasant surprise. It made me think of my ROTC days in college. Our Air Force Colonel was stationed in Thailand for several years and brought one of his friends, a General from Thailand, to talk to us. As a hick from a small farm in North Dakota, I was impressed. Watching the two officers kidding around personalized the world of life in the military so I could see it was more than polished shoes and brass buttons.

The boat tour ended at lunch time 1:00 pm which was a pleasant buffet of Asian food, most of which was very good to our taste. Then, starting an hour later, we began a bus tour to a temple which entailed much walking and was not nearly as fascinating as the tour-guide tried to make it. They are Buddhists and seem to spend their treasure and time building temples and palaces for the king whom they speak of almost as a god.

The tour-guide promised to take a group shopping which turned out to be a very bad experience in that she took us to a place run by her brother-in-law or some other group with influence over her. Getting back to the hotel, we didn't go with the group for the dinner and traditional Thai dancing girls at a fancy hotel. We went shopping at the Jim Thompson silk store. Claudia knew of this store from her trip here twenty years ago.

We finished shopping and went back to the hotel where the concierge guided us to a Thai restaurant on the second floor. Then, on the way to dinner, we walked by a men's tailor shop. I had been determined to get a suit or a blazer, for sure, either in Bangkok or Hong Kong. As we reviewed the fabrics and workmanship of this shop, we were impressed. I told him I was looking for a blue blazer and he told us that everything was made to order; however, he did have a jacket he made for somebody else who didn't take it. He said was close to my size. Well, it was nearly perfect except the sleeves were a little long. He informed us that it was no problem, even though we were leaving at seven in the morning and it now was ten at night, he would have it ready for us the next morning. Now that's service. We were so impressed I bought two more suits that would be shipped back to our house in the states. In the morning the jacket was ready and when we got home the other suits were there also. Sometimes when you find something this wonderful and cheap, you have to go for it.

The shopping places closed at ten then we then went to eat at the Thai restaurant which was a delight. We quizzed the waitress a little about her personal life. We found out she was single, lived in her own place and was from a family of one older brother and two younger ones. The youngest was away and because that's all the information she was willing to say about the youngest, it made Claudia wonder if he had gotten into trouble or something.

The next day was spent viewing the beautiful temples and palaces. These building are fabulous with tile roofs, golden touches and intricate decorations that create their distinctive Thai traditional style.

After two days, we were tired of walking and were glad to be home; the ship now feels like home.

04/07/2009 4:02 pm

Bangkok temple

04/07/2009 6.53 pm

Bangkok temple

Bangkok shoping area

Bangkok palace

CHAPTER 12

SAIGON, VIETNAM

Here we selected an excursion that took us by bus from the port city to Saigon which is about 50 miles away and was scheduled to take two hours. It turned out to be a three hour trip in the early morning and five hour trip coming home in rush hour in a rattle trap bus.

The people were aggressive to the point of being rude. The bus driver couldn't even enter traffic at one place. Where most countries cater to tourists, these people seemed to despise us and Saigon looked like it — there were very few tourists. I know I'm not going back. It is difficult for me to make a blanket condemnation of any place because I know there are numerous people who tried their best to make ours a pleasant trip. For instance, the young tour-guide on the bus on the way home tried to hand out a customer satisfaction survey of sorts, which most people refused. I took one and it was definitely put together by someone who knew how to phrase questions like, "Have you stopped beating your wife yet?" I filled it out because he explained it was for his studies or something like that. I don't think anyone on the bus that ever fought traffic had anything but sympathy for the driver. He had a deadline to get us back to the ship and probably was shot at sunrise for not achieving this goal. I hope I am not being too melodramatic, however, as is customary when you leave such a bus, a tip for the driver and tour-guide is customary. I gave him a $5 bill and when he opened his hand I could see he had practically nothing in it. He looked at me in astonishment and stopped talking on his cell phone long enough to thank me in his language and bow his head. I was the only person he did that to. The poor bastard, what could he do about the traffic? I believe he did his level best.

We shopped at a market where the sellers hound you half to death. The taxi that took us there and back said the trip would cost $5 and then demanded $10 once we got to our destination. We got some clothing items and two knock-off watches that we had wanted for some time, a "Rado" for me and a "Chanel" for Claudia. Claudia also got two suitcases which we will need to get our loot back home and we are not even half-way through our trip yet.

One thing we, I should say, Claudia has, observed about the fabric in Asia is that the cotton they use is very finely spun; it almost has a silky feel to it. I bought two shirts that I thought were silk until she told me differently; I got them anyway because they were so light and airy and believe me, here no matter where you go it is hot and you sweat — a lot.

No matter how hard I tried, I couldn't help but think of all the money we poured into Vietnam during the sixties and seventies and there appears to be absolutely nothing to show for it. The roads are terrible and the infrastructure looks like nothing has been done since we left forty years ago. We drove by miles and miles of rice paddies which seemed to be productive but there was a tinge of poverty and oppression that was disturbing.

The picture of the house we took shows a typical Vietnamese house, they are tall and narrow, apparently to fit on small lots. They look unusual to our western eyes.

04/10/2009 1:57 pm

Vietnam house

Vietnam checkpoint

CHAPTER 13

BORNEO, INDONESIA

We spent a short Easter Sunday afternoon on this stop on an island is called Saba—it is a very progressive place. We saw a large, well-maintained and impressive university on our outing. It was quite a distinguished campus facility and one we had never heard of which shows our ignorance of their culture.

Our female tour-guide was an interesting person; she chattered constantly and was obsessed with the fact that one of the monkey species on the island has a rather long penis. It remains erect all the time and he uses it frequently on the group of females he has in his harem of a dozen or so. We were not quite sure what to make of her and this fetish or whatever you might call it but you never know what useless information you learn on these trips.

The bus stopped at a pier where we boarded an open raft with a roof; it held twenty five people. The tour-guide told us about the river and how the government has now prohibited the use of house-boats, the traditional form of housing for these people. The damage and deaths that occur whenever a storm hits the area, which is frequent, has forced the new rules for the people's protection. These fishermen and their families have been furnished apartments close to the water but up away from the river. She also pointed out their tsunami guard…a dense thicket of mangrove trees that grow along the river. These trees form a natural barrier about two hundred feet wide and so thick you can't see through them. They have a massive root system and even if the water crashed into them, they do not become dislodged; they just bend and remain. While we were moving up and down the river, the guide, with the help of a few passengers, baited and threw out six crab traps; when we checked them an hour later we had only one crab.

We signed up for this tour because it advertised a trip through a batik factory which turned out to be nothing but an open-air shelter with a roof and some tables. Here each of us water-colored an image on a 12 by 14 piece of material; this is something that kids would do to keep busy on a non-school day. The real process of making a batik cloth starts with a piece of material that has a pattern outline pressed into it in wax. Then the designer, us, paint in the center of the design; it is then dried. The color we used did not stick to the outlined areas which left the cloth colored but when done professionally they are beautiful; the women on the cruise each had to have several. The ones we painted here we threw away because they were so crude looking.

After the fishing we tasted some of their local food in a café of sorts where you sit on the floor on a mat, we were asked to remove our shoes before entering. Then we went to a pottery factory and gift/tourist trap. The prices were great and I bought a small object that holds two letter-opener-swords that are brass and beautifully decorated with chains and inscriptions.

We came back to the ship, showered as is the usual procedure, because you sweat profusely in the heat. We rested and dressed "Smart Casual" for dinner, but when we got to the elevator we saw everybody in formal attire which sent us scurrying back to the stateroom and re-dressing in formal duds. We switched tables in the dining room this week and now we have new table with a couple from Athens, Georgia. He is a Veterinary Doctor who is a professor that teaches at the University of Georgia, now semi-retired. We also have a single, retired teacher from Brooklyn, New York. I think he is one of the many people who has never married, lives alone and is content with his life. I worked and lived in New York and knew several such people. Some have cats or dogs; they are their family. Then we had a Kiwi, a spinster lady from New Zealand, also a retired teacher. This was our table until we got to Japan where the two single people got off the ship and for the remainder of the cruise there were just four of us at the table for six. All were very pleasant company and we enjoyed many a dinner conversation together.

On Monday we had a Mariner Party. The Mariner Club is comprised of those of us who have traveled on more than one cruise with the Holland America Cruise Line. This one is a brunch; most events are just drinks and canapés. With 62 days on this cruise we are veteran mariners, the whole club is a sales pitch to "come again", but we enjoyed the event nevertheless. We also got a brass medal on a blue ribbon to hang around our necks to show we have 100 days of sailing with this cruise line—yippee.

04/12/2009 5:15 pm

Boroneo Mosque

04/12/2009 6:09 pm

Boroneo boat

47

CHAPTER 14

PORTO PRINCESA CITY, PHILIPPINES

This is the first port of call in the Philippine Islands. We went ashore about noon, walked to the taxi pool and hired a guy with a motorcycle. These taxis are motorcycles that have an attached side-car all under one roof that they obviously have made themselves from whatever materials they find. They call them tricycles and the streets are full of them as they are the main mode of transportation. Wend was our driver and he took us around to the half dozen spots we knew to see and then he showed us a few other things we didn't know about. We drove and drove looking for the place recommended by the ship's tour-guide as the best place to shop. We finally found it after Wend inquired half a dozen times. One thing was for sure, that shop certainly had good merchandise with unbelievable prices. Claudia bought some wonderful shell and wooden jewelry; notable was a superbly crafted mother-of-pearl necklace which she treasures.

One thing I noticed about this place was that the fishing boats all had inboard motors; I didn't see one outboard. I always have an eye for the mechanics of things; I guess it's a guy thing. However, on an island where the major mode of land transportation is a bunch of rickety motorcycles with flimsily attached side cars, I find it amazing that the boats have inboard engines. It is a much more expensive way to propel small water craft.

We shopped at their two story mall; it was a grocery store on the ground level and on the second floor they sold everything from clothing to bicycles. I got an electric three way adapter for the ship's cabin which has only one easy-to-get- at electric plug. This allowed me to plug in the camera charger, the cell phone and the laptop at the same time. Claudia commented that we make our little stateroom homier and handier all the time.

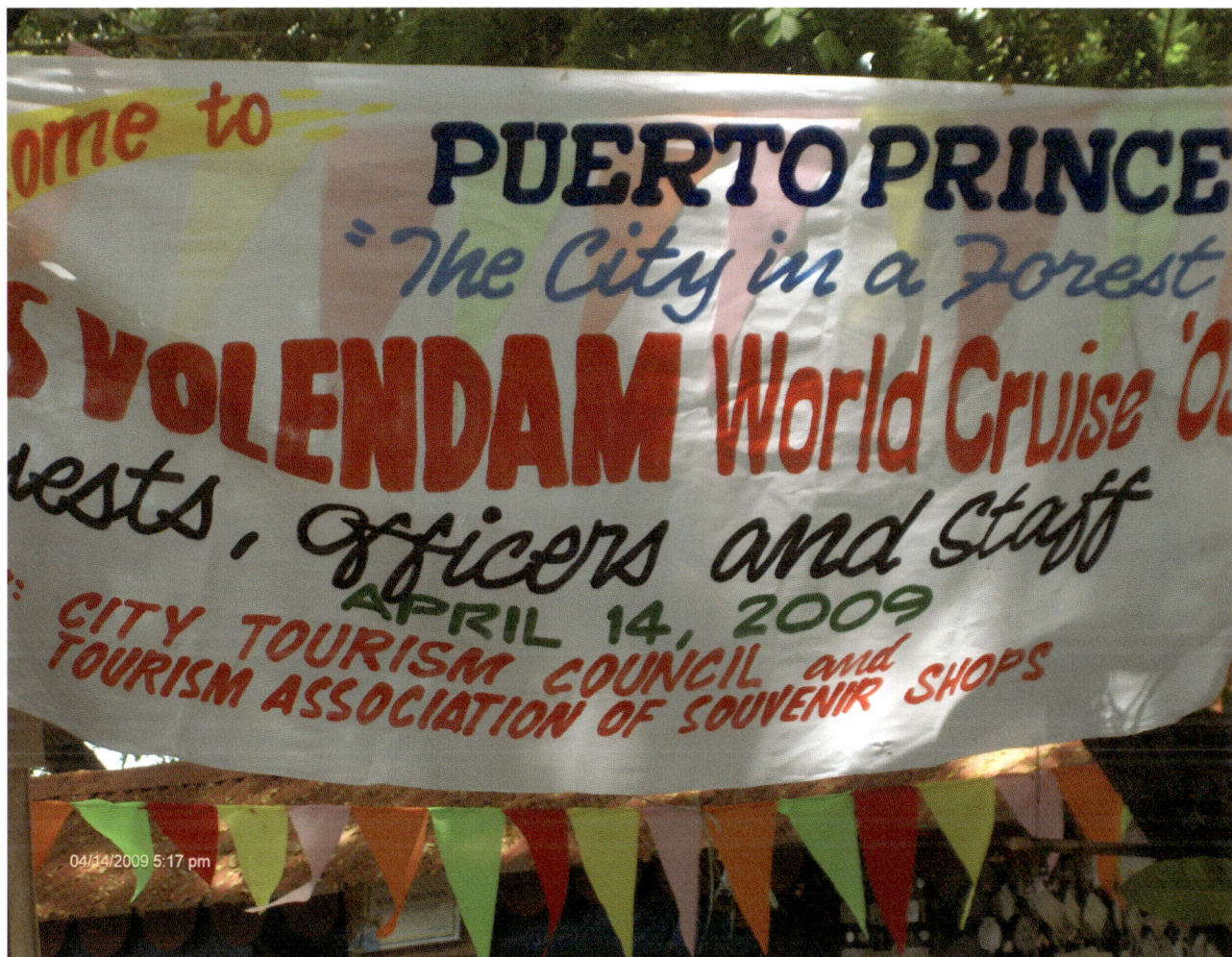

Philipines Puerto Princesa

CHAPTER 15
MANILA & CORREGIDOR, THE PHILIPPINES

Early morning today I went to Corregidor which is the sight of the horrific battles General MacArthur's troops fought against the Japanese in WWII. Claudia went on a separate city tour to a nearby town which took the group around the town and to a museum that contained part of Imelda Marcos' huge shoe collection.

The road to Corregidor was first a bus ride through the harbor district, then on to a catamaran boat that took the 150 of us the 26 miles across the Manila harbor to the island of Corregidor. Once there, we loaded up in trolley cars that before WWII rode on a track all over the island; now they have been converted to rubber tires so we went on roads. We squeezed five men onto hard wooden benches designed to hold four midgets and went bouncing along the ten or so miles around the island.

We had a 73 year old native man as a guide and had the tour lasted another hour there would have been another casualty on the island to add the thousands who died here during the war. A group of us would have strangled him. He blathered about every irrelevant thing that ever happened to him including the ghosts he had seen here on the island but he did have some good information, if you quizzed him. So the lot of us managed to ask questions to keep him on topic.

Our group started at the tunnel system that the U.S. Army had dug starting in 1922 when the Philippines came under the U.S. protection. One tunnel, as one of my pictures shows was finished in 1932. It took ten years to dig all the tunnels, not exactly a speed record, but it was quite an extensive tunnel labyrinth, as shown in the pictures. The commentator who conducted the tour through the tunnel pointed out that at one time 8,000 troops and a handful of Philippine nurses all lived in the tunnel complex when the Japanese were bombing the island.

The sad saga continued; in May of 1942 the island was surrendered to the Japanese and the some 4,000 of the defenders were moved to Manila and marched through the streets. The remaining 7,000 defenders were dispersed to various prison camps but the majority were moved to the mainland and forced into a death march to the prison camps. Some 5,000 soldiers and civilian defenders of Corregidor, including many women, died. This is in addition to 20,000 American, Australian and Philippine defenders of Luzon, who perished in the infamous Bataan death march some weeks earlier. The various guides throughout the day claimed that the Japanese visitors, who have their own guides, are told that the war in the pacific was to liberate these people from the expansion of Western Civilization. Also notable on the tour were various cliffs where the guides said many Japanese jumped to their deaths rather than be captured by the allies when the island was retaken in 1944.

After the extensive tour through the tunnel system we stopped for lunch at a hilltop hotel and restaurant and then drove around, touring the island and stopping at bombed out buildings and gun emplacements. We were told that the island has been left as it was when the war ended as a war memorial and museum. The guide pointed out Macarthur's headquarters before the bombing and the harbor from which he escaped to Australia. Apparently he was nearly killed on the beach because the navy and army fought over whose dock would be used; such goes inter-service rivalries then, now and always.

There were several huge, ten ton 12-inch mortars and a half-dozen long range guns called "shore guns" used to defend against oncoming ships. These were the mainstay of the island's defense. There were also two such long range guns that had never gotten into place before hostilities started; they now lay in place where the army left them at the time of the surrender. Of particular interest to me was the manufacture date stamped on the end of the barrel; the dates were all in the 1890's. So in 1942 we were using guns made in the 19th century. Maybe those big guns were not that much different by then; they were massive and apparently worked very well but weren't enough to save the island. One story tells that the first time the guns were fired in tests they shattered the windows on the island. When surrender was imminent, we were told that the firing mechanisms were removed and thrown in the ocean to prevent the enemy from using them. Apparently the Japanese tortured the soldiers until they told where the mechanisms were dumped and then they dove down and found one.

There was a museum on the island that contained all the associated details of the events during the war. Someone in the group asked, "How many people lived on the island?" The answer was approximately 300, but no families. The old guide said that women and the kids made the island too messy so the workers lived on the mainland and only worked on the island, they lived in dormitory type of accommodations if they stayed over night.

Corrdgidor tunnel

me and big gun

bombed out building

PACIFIC WAR MEMORIA

ERECTED TO THE FILIPINO AND AMERICAN FIGHTING MEN WHO
GAVE THEIR LIVES TO WIN THE LAND, SEA AND AIR VICTORIES
WHICH RESTORED FREEDOM AND PEACE TO THE PACIFIC OCEAN AREA

04/16/2009 5:26 pm

war museum sign

CHAPTER 16

HONG KONG

Moving through the ship channel with the huge skyscrapers crowded on either side reminded me of being in New York City for the first time, an experience that was almost incomprehensible for a kid from a farm in North Dakota. I had seen pictures and movies of the city, but not until I actually stood on the streets looking up could I fathom the majesty of it all. Hong Kong had the same effect on me. I follow financial markets every day of which Hong Kong is a significant player, but nothing I knew about the city from the media prepared me for the experience of seeing it first hand.

I have heard of the majesty of Hong Kong for years; I even had a young man that worked for me as an auditor move there after being assigned there for two years with our company. He loved it, and as far as I know, is still there. I can understand his fascination.

We took a tour of the highlights of the city the one day we were there and my first impression was of the crowded conditions; but I had never realized the steep mountain environment of the region. Any spot that isn't sheer cliff is built up fifty stories high and those on the mountains are three to five stories high. The view from the top of Victoria Mountain is a spectacular panorama of the city.

A young woman who was our tour-guide showed us the highlights of the city and explained to us the facts of living in the most densely populated parcel of land on the planet. She told us of her childhood, growing up in a four hundred square foot apartment shared by ten people, her four siblings, two grand parents, an uncle and of course her parents. Her parents, uncle and grandfather worked, leaving grandma in charge of the home. She told us she helped from the time she was able to walk, especially being the only daughter and second in birth order. The heavy responsibilities of chasing after younger brothers often fell to her as grandma aged. Eventually at age ten she did most of the fetching, cleaning and some cooking.

Our day over, I stood on the balcony of our stateroom and watched our departure. There was a heavy mist, not quite fog, not quite rain, that hung over the Hong Kong harbor as our ship slowly moved between the massive skyscrapers. The low sound of ships' fog horns moaned in the dusk as darkness slipped over the area. It was an eerie scene, like in an old mystery movie where someone is sneaking around the harbor in a trench coat with his collar pulled up and a hat scrunched down, ready to stab someone in the back before someone stabbed him. These were the kinds of things we imagined as kids, listening to a radio show, where your imagination created images far more vivid than any movie set or TV show.

The lights soon owned the night, twinkling their radiance in what seemed like an undeclared war between the opposite sides of the harbor. The reflections in the water made it look like a separate city existed in the space between the shores. My face was moist from the dew as we sped up and the city slowly disappeared in the fog, continuing the myth-like appearance. So did Hong Kong really exist or was it like Brigadoon of Scottish folklore, only visible once every one hundred years before it again disappears in the fog? However, for the villagers of Brigadoon each hundred years seems just like one night. They made a covenant with God to save their village on the eve of destruction by enemies. The spell stays in effect only as long as no one ever leaves the village—or else Brigadoon will disappear in the fog forever.

Hong Kong

old city Hong Kong

CHAPTER 17

OUR SAGA OF THE SOUTH PACIFIC

When we decided to write this book we considered it would be a travelogue of the sights and scenery of our tour through areas of the world mostly new to us. This was our first experience of seeing life in the nations that make up the South Pacific region and the Asian Tiger Economies. Claudia was in China in 1979 so she was ready to see what changes had occurred; she had been in Japan several times as her daughter worked there as a teacher for three years.

Even within one month's time awareness of the reality of life in many of these countries was evident by what you see while you are moving between the notable tourist sights of palaces, temples and tourist-trap gift shops. What you come face to face with is the living conditions of poor people, of which there are millions. Whether it is the ramshackle house you look into—in fact through—where women sit tending children or cooking food on an outside hearth with a few pieces of tin as a roof, or staring into the sunken eyes of an emaciated five year old girl tugging your pant leg, begging you to buy something from her…its heart breaking.

The crew members on our ship were from several of these Asian countries, primarily Indonesia and the Philippines. We, mostly Claudia, quizzed them about their lives and homelands. They sign a contract with a cruise company to work eight months to a year without going home; they make about one thousand dollars a month. This is multiple times what they could make in their home countries even if they could find a job, so they tell us. This is the price of survival for them, not that they are the only ones that ever lived like that in the history of the world. Military people and others are often separated from their homes for long periods of time also, but in these people's case it is their only option, there is no social security, no safety net and very few jobs available for young people.

The other thing we learned was that most of the young guys on the ship have wives and kids at home. The cruise ships use nearly all young men, even for housekeeping, because on cruise ships the crew also does the luggage handling and loading and distributing heavy cases of supplies. These jobs are too heavy for women as a bar waitress, one of the few women we met, informed us. She told us that even the dining room work involved carrying huge trays of food from the kitchen often up flights of stairs or escalators which is extremely difficult, even for the males. Naturally many of the young people we talked to were a little homesick, but they felt lucky to be working and intended to sign up again for future tours.

When we were in the ports of the countries where the crew is from, the families would come to visit the ship and a big festive buffet was provided for them. Our stateroom attendant was Filipino as were many of his fellow workers. When we docked, the pier was a mass of humanity, all relatives of the crew. Our attendant told us the day before that he needed to be finished making up our cabin by 11:00 am so he could join his family. The cruise line seemed to be very nice to these people and they pretty much had the run of the ship as we saw them everywhere, touring the areas where the particular crew members worked. We got to meet some of our attendant's family as we were coming back to our stateroom.

Back to our travels, throughout Asia the things we witnessed things like a woman in a house on a canal scooping up water out of the canal and bathing a baby in it. I later asked what they do with the sewage in this city and the answer was it goes in the canal and they rely on the tide to carry it out to sea; I didn't want to know where they get their drinking water.

We saw barely-standing shacks at the end of rice paddies with kids running around playing and laundry hanging on a line with men standing in knee deep water working the rice fields. Many village shops we visited especially the ones off the main tourist paths often are also the homes of the owners evidenced by the smells of cooking and children's toys laying around. Some of the shops are apparently multi-generational, as you see elders working at various activities or often tending the young while the middle age people work with customers. The youngsters starting at about the age of ten often act as interrupters as they learn English in school.

Interestingly we observed that most of these people, although they have little, seem generally happy, live normal lives, work hard all week, pray to their god and raise their children to be respectful decent humans whom they hope to educate to have a better life than they have.

They indeed are like us in so many ways; we observed many holidays with backyards and picnic areas crowded with groups, some huge groups of family gatherings. One place, I don't remember where, there was a children's table loaded with McDonald's Happy Meals. Some things seem universal, I remember a time when I was working in Panama City the director of the computer systems department invited me to go with his family for Sunday brunch. In Panama there are still the huge country club type facilities one would associate with nineteenth century colonization. They are cabana style facilities replete with rattan furniture surrounding elegant tables covered with white tablecloths there are ballrooms with gloved waiters standing by to fulfill your every request. My host and his delightful wife had three children; the youngest was about four years old, on our way to brunch we had to stop by a McDonalds to pick up a Happy Meal for him.

We now are going to be entering a different Asia…China and Japan…where the Tiger Economies are much more aggressive and developed than where we have traveled, save for Australia. It has been said that globalization has done more to raise the standard of living around the world than anything in history; it looks like we still have a ways to go. One can only hope the next generation of world citizens can achieve more to help their children and grand children. Hopefully, we can accomplish this without destroying the standard of living we have in the developed world; a formidable task I fear, and hopefully we in the US will have more to export than McDonalds.

CHAPTER 18

SHANGHAI CHINA

Shanghai is one hell of a busy place. Our ship docked on the Huangpu River that has nearly bow to stern barges moving up and down the river hauling everything from sand to fuel, with lots of coal; they must be supplying electric plants. The streets are just as busy and no one would think there is any kind of recession going on elsewhere. They are building everything and everywhere you look. "Expo China In 2010" is splashed all over. There is even a huge ship with a 30 foot wide 20 foot high movie screen moving up and down the river advertising it and all the sponsors' products describing the event.

The ship's tour-lecturer states in his discussion of Shanghai, that money is pouring in from everywhere. This appears to be an understatement. The building cranes are crowded so close together they interfere with each other.

We first went to a museum of China's history of jade, furniture, sculpture and other objects made from jade and of course there were gift shops.

Then we went to the old market part of town, which has been rebuilt within the last fifty years to resemble an ancient market. The tour ended with a visit to a silk manufacturing shop. This incredible operation shows how they draw the silk from the worms. First they feed the worm until it makes a cocoon where it spins itself into a silk wrap from which it will metamorphose into a butterfly. When the worm finishes the spinning process, they bake it inside its shell, killing it. Then they catch the silk strands and un-spin it with a machine that rewraps the strands onto spools that are then used for making fabric. We watched some women make comforters from the silk that is matted and can't be separated into strands, so they leave it in clumps which they stretch between four women to fit the comforter they are making. Guess what? We bought one! They shrink wrapped it to make it easy to carry, sort of.

The view from our ship balcony faces what they call the new city where the bulk of the new buildings are going up. The old part of town is mostly under going renovations, which are also extensive.

The evening of the first day we went into the city for a performance of a troop of Chinese acrobats which was a wonderful event. The performers were more than half women; the men tumbled and the women did balancing acts. One girl balanced a chandelier on her foot, sticking up in the air and was able to twist herself from her back to her stomach while still holding the thing on her foot. Then she completed the rollover to her back again, so she rotated her body completely around while balancing the chandelier on her foot. Others balanced themselves on chairs stacked up six high. One balanced a glass on her head and hands and one on a mechanism in her mouth; then she proceeded to sit down and stand up while balancing all these. Of course the men jumped through hoops at different heights even while a group of four hoops rotated on a table and each of the eight of them would jump through them as it moved around. Amazing, even Cirque Du Soleil doesn't compare.

There were also comic acts; one where a knife thrower pitched knives at the traditional wall where the person stands and the knives are thrown all around him. In this show a cowardly assistant always ran away at just the last minute. Then they got a volunteer from the audience to stand against the target, blindfolded him and strapped him in so he couldn't move. The knife thrower would yell as though he was throwing the knife so the victim assumed he was throwing the knife; however, he never did. The assistant would jam the knife in the target by the victim in rhythm with the yell from the thrower. The victim never knew the difference; he thought the knife was thrown from the distance…it was pretty funny.

They had magicians and a guy that threw heavy porcelain planters up in the air and caught them on his neck just behind his head or spun them around on the top of his head. Of course pretty assistant girls, beautifully dressed, were part of it all.

The second day we got up late and decided not to go on the second tour we had purchased. Instead we took a taxi into the main shopping square and just kicked around and wound up in a cosmetic store where they sold Claudia some eye make-up. While I was waiting a couple of aggressive, but pleasant, sales girls started fooling around smearing stuff on my eyes and face and sold me some stuff too. I don't know if it works but it was fun trying to communicate with them and listen to them trying to convince me their product was great. This event was as entertaining as anything I've done so far.

At that same shop there was one girl that had absolute porcelain skin; she looked like a China doll. I had fun teasing her while I waited for Claudia, she was very pleasant…she had never heard of Texas or Houston.

An interesting side note to China was how aware many of the young men were about the US pro-basketball teams. When we would mention Houston they would tell us about the last game or what kind of season the team was having. They all seemed to have favorite teams even though you would expect them to be a follower of Yao Ming, the seven foot Chinese man that plays for the Houston Rockets. Claudia said he is the son of a man and woman both of whom are professional basketball players in China. Yao Ming was the athlete who held the Chinese flag in the 2008 Summer Olympics. He and his parents also have a restaurant in Houston.

It is nearly dark now on the last night in Shanghai and the lights are coming on and the traffic on the river is so beautiful and interesting, actually inspiring. Everyone is working so hard building, repairing and bustling about.

There is a low bridge crossing the river we are on and the ships must go under it coming in and leaving. We came in nose first and had to turn the ship around to leave the same way. When the ship was crossways in the river there were only a few feet of clearance front and back. Several patrol boats closed off traffic on the river and some around the ship, watching to make sure all was clear until we completed our turn. Next was the bridge the ship had only a few feet of clearance even when we left at low tide. Everyone was watching from the top deck and the verandas as we made these complex maneuvers. Even though the passengers had nothing to do with driving the ship by midnight when we got through all the challenges everybody was tired and ready for bed. Next we were off to Beijing and the Great Wall.

Shanghai river traffic

Shanghai TV tower

Shanghai consturction

CHAPTER 19

Two Days at Sea

We have two days at sea and time to catch up on much-needed rest. The constant travel, even though there are one day breaks from time to time, still wears you down and more rest is welcome. These are the days I spend writing trying to stay caught up with all the places we just visited. Claudia tends to our needs: clothing, hair, nails and reviewing gifts and packing them, etc. We are moving into cooler climates now, so she had me pull the suitcases out from under the bed where she took out warmer clothes and packed up the tropical clothing. She is a wonder in how she keeps track of all the clothing items and which pieces go together and where they are — it's amazing.

The ship lecturers are also busy on these days because everybody is on the ship so the talks are scheduled every day. Additionally, we might watch the latest movie or do some reading but definitely review the schedule for the upcoming days. I keep up with the home-front via email. The ship has a satellite internet connection and in most places it worked, but was extremely slow in the middle of the ocean, far from land. Their internet equipment use connections of any land-based facilities when we are at port or near land. On the open sea the link is through satellite and it must be the oldest, slowest one up there, maybe Sputnik, the first one the Russians put up in 1957.

We got two new lecturers for the last twenty days of the cruise. One had pictures and maps explaining the history of the Bering Sea and the Russian, Vitus Bering, who discovered it for Russia and for whom it is named. The other is a photographer, a naturalist, who displayed his extensive pictures and described the wildlife in this area of the Northern Pacific and the Aleutian Islands.

The other daily activities include breakfast, always in our stateroom, and lunch whenever we want it; on these days we usually have formal nights. These become more interesting after we have stopped at the various ports where the ladies buy dresses of local design. Some are magnificent and others interesting. When West meets East in a dress shop, it's a sure thing there will be a purchase. The one thing I noticed was the women in these cultures, of all ages, wear dresses well above the knee. They wear heavy stockings under it, almost like leggings. It really is nice and it does give an older lady a real boost in terms of looks, compared to their Western women counterparts who wear long dresses to cover their legs. This is because they don't think their legs are pretty enough to show anymore; a situation made worse by the trend of ladies not wearing stockings these days.

CHAPTER 20

BEIJING, CHINA

Beijing is about 100 miles from the port where the ship docked. However, the points of interest, The Forbidden City and Tian'anmen Square are located in Beijing and one section of the Great Wall is within an hour's drive from Beijing. Thus there were two options for the two days the ship was docked here: you could ride on the bus each day to see one place and return to the ship that night and ride to the other the next day; or you could stay in a hotel in Beijing overnight which saved some seven hours of driving time over the two days. We selected the overnight stay in Beijing.

The Forbidden City and Tiananmen Square were big and involved an enormous amount of walking. As for these places, I will revert to the saying I think is attributed to Mark Twain, "That's the sort of thing you'll like, if you like that sort of thing." Claudia loved it. The palaces are mammoth and the grounds the size of small cities. It was used as a parade ground, a place to address masses of people and to impress 15th to 19th century visitors.

The next day Claudia, following the advice from one of her shipmate lady-friends, worked on our tour-guide and, although it was not on the schedule, she talked the driver into taking us past the Bird's Nest Stadium. This is the building that looks like a huge, shiny steel, upside down bird nest and it was where many of the summer Olympics events of 2008 were held. It was unfortunate that the other groups didn't go by it, because it was not that far off the road to the Great Wall from Beijing and is a far more interesting structure then many of the ancient sites we visited. Claudia doesn't think so, but I think in a hundred years from now it will probably be the greatest tourist attraction…it isn't old enough yet.

The Great Wall is an incredible structure and to think of it being built thousands of miles across china is truly mind boggling. The area of this wall that we visited extended up the side of a mountain for about a half mile. It was the challenge of the day to get to the top. Claudia and I had no intention of going that far but did go about a quarter of the way…you can't come all this way and not do some of it. That was enough for us; then when we started coming down my dear little Claudia slipped on the steps and fell backwards — it was a terrible fall. We had been holding hands but lost our grip — it just happened so fast. She slipped or missed the step. She spun around and landed on her butt with her right arm extended to defend against the fall. I could imagine a broken hip or wrist or arm. I bent down to her instantly trying to comfort her and she started to cry. I asked if she was hurt and she just cried. By this time at least twenty people had gathered around and wanted to help. Several men got together and offered to carry her down. They showed me how two guys hold hands and the injured person sits on their arms with her arms around their necks. They used one of their women to demonstrate. One has to assume that's the instant stretcher China style…very sensible. Often that might be the only option. She and I soon determined that she could move her legs and arms without extreme pain, so I was pretty sure nothing was broken. Her wrist was badly sprained and her butt hurt but she was able to get up with help from me and several by-standers. She was now able to walk and my poor baby was embarrassed and didn't want anybody else to help. I held her left arm and we started down the steps on our own. Several of the bystanders followed us all the way to the bottom, which was extremely thoughtful. I bowed to them and thanked them in English and they bowed back several times responding in Chinese and then went back to their activities. It gave me an appreciation of the kindness and neighborliness of the Chinese people that I will never forget. These people weren't tour-guides or officials watching out for tourists; they were just ordinary people, probably local tourists themselves. They just did it out of concern for another human being. If only countries' relations could be handled at this level, the world would be a different place.

We got back on the bus and got to the ship just before dark and sailing time; Claudia was better after some pain pills and a good night's rest. The wrist was tender for more than a week and, of course her bottom, was black and blue but I can't believe how lucky we were and shudder to think of how bad it could have been. We later heard a story of a woman who, on this same trip, fell getting off the bus and had to be taken to a hospital and air ambulanced home. We met another man who broke his wrist falling on a flat level sidewalk — getting old is hell. The worst is you have to hang around with all these other old people. One thing that has impressed me about us oldsters is our resilience and compassion for each other. We might be a little older than once we were but we still got some good miles left. So now we watch out for one another, sympathize any injuries and make the best of any situation — fully aware that others have it worse.

04/25/2009 7:41 pm

Bejeing Forbiden City

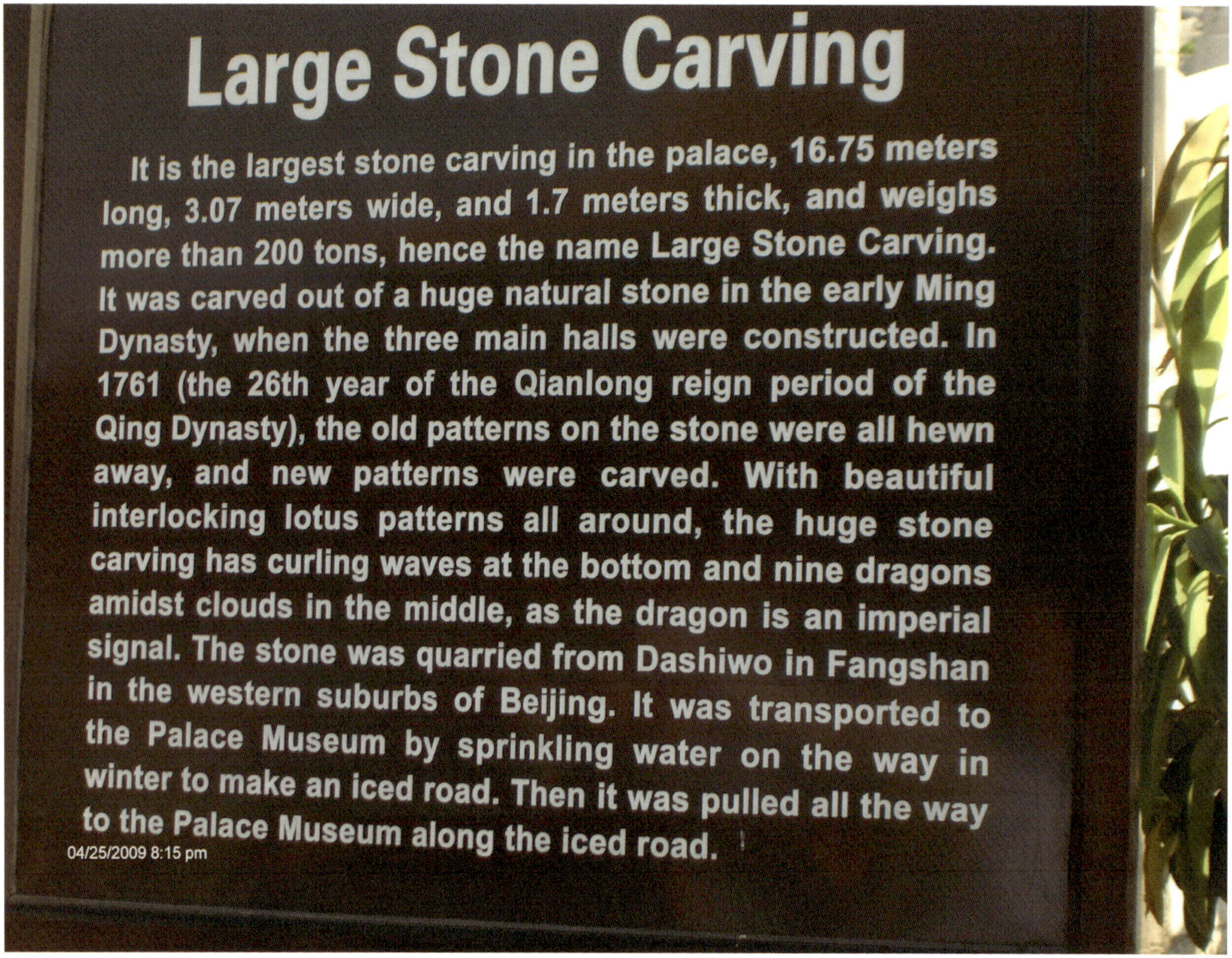

Large Stone Carving

It is the largest stone carving in the palace, 16.75 meters long, 3.07 meters wide, and 1.7 meters thick, and weighs more than 200 tons, hence the name Large Stone Carving. It was carved out of a huge natural stone in the early Ming Dynasty, when the three main halls were constructed. In 1761 (the 26th year of the Qianlong reign period of the Qing Dynasty), the old patterns on the stone were all hewn away, and new patterns were carved. With beautiful interlocking lotus patterns all around, the huge stone carving has curling waves at the bottom and nine dragons amidst clouds in the middle, as the dragon is an imperial signal. The stone was quarried from Dashiwo in Fangshan in the western suburbs of Beijing. It was transported to the Palace Museum by sprinkling water on the way in winter to make an iced road. Then it was pulled all the way to the Palace Museum along the iced road.

04/25/2009 8:15 pm

Bejeing carving sign

Bejeing stone carving

Chinese sign

04/26/2009 11:06 am

Olympic stadium 'Bird Nest'

China's Disney Land now closed

The Great Wall

CHAPTER 21

DALIAN, CHINA

This is our last stop in China and we have been discussing our impressions of the people and their country's progress. The friendliness and courtesy shown to us was exemplary, as witnessed by the throng that seemingly out of instinct, rushed to our aid when Claudia fell — they didn't just stand by and watch, not wanting to get involved — more then a dozen people jammed in around us wanting to assist. As a people, the Chinese are good looking, well dressed, ambitious and seemingly willing to do anything to survive. They are looking for an increased standard of living and we think they are about at the point the U.S. was 50 years ago. They live on little, save a lot and are seemingly content with their lot in life. They remember how bad things were just a generation ago, like people in the U.S. after the depression of the nineteen thirties. Whatever forces are at work to manage their economy, the country is brimming with construction and their economic growth hovers around ten percent per year. We were informed that in the current economic slow down they had implemented a government works project where each person was paid for cleaning up a certain area, about one square block; thus, the unemployed have a job and an income and the city is improved as well.

We visited the downtown and, because we were tired, we only went to the "Friendship Store" which is China's government owned Department Store. There were no bargains but the quality was good. We had quite a time; no one spoke or understood English on any of the eight floors where we shopped. If we had a question, a sales person would run to find someone who could understand English and even those we could barely communicate with. When we first got there I tried to establish the exchange rate on money, so we would know for sure what we were paying for things. It was about seven Yuans to the dollar; they couldn't explain the price in English, so they would show us with a calculator what the price was and especially where discounts applied. Claudia bought a few things including a purse, her second choice, because she and another lady both put their hands on one at the same time. The other lady won, but the two sort of became friends over the deal because when they saw each other on the ship afterwards they had a laugh about it. Your new friendships on these cruises are often made in just such ways, the people at your dinner table, those you sit next to on land excursions or those you just meet.

We did have a problem or an inconvenience getting back on the ship. Instead of the Chinese officials having a table at the bottom of the loading ramp to check whatever they wanted, from your room key to the ship, a driver's license or some other government issued ID card. In this case they checked our bags to see what we had in them; no one we knew figured out what they were looking for. Anyway they dropped us off at the official building used for clearing merchant ships which was some distance from our ship. So we got off one bus stood in a long line as they slowly looked through our bags; then we boarded another bus that dropped us off at the ship's loading ramp. One of the officers of the ship was there yelling at the officials stating, "We've got 600 people that will be coming through here in the next hour and they need to get through in that amount of time." As far as I could figure out the system stood because those I talked to who came aboard after us also had to go through that system and we didn't leave for three more hours.

CHAPTER 22

CHEJU, KOREA

We split up today; I went on a tour of a mountain crater and some local villages while Claudia went to a folk music performance and shopping tour. The music she heard was the same as the group that played on the dock where we got off the ship; it was awful, just banging on drums and metal pans; we are just not fans of drums. When I heard it out the window I thought it was guys working in the foundry on the dock pounding metal into shape. Worse, her shopping trip was to the local mall where only high end merchandise was for sale and the ladies' discussing the prices discovered things cost much more than in the states. Claudia did manage to buy a silk hat at a market where they had the same drum pounding entertainment; the ships daily program said it was a college group that was performing for us.

My tour was some better, except for a climb up a mountain to look at a dry crater lake, but it was a good view of the island and the bus took us all but the last 100 yards. My tour of the ancient villages was interesting in that people still live in these houses. They are low ceiling structures with thatched roofs, but they had running water, refrigerators and television. The units were small, about twenty feet square. I didn't get to see the plumbing setup but I assume they had indoor modern bathroom facilities because of the lack of outhouses. I got one picture of a young man, maybe fourteen; I had been poking around near the front door of this house to get a picture and then when I briefly looked the other way, a teenage boy suddenly appeared standing in front of me. I was standing on the walk, in his way, as he was coming out of this house. He was dressed as any well-dressed teenager from a major western city would be. I indicated I wanted to take his picture. He just stood there but I could tell he only did it out of politeness. The instant I snapped the camera he bolted out to the street. He joined a dozen other boys all dressed similarly; they ran off joking and jibing as boys do. It was about noon so they probably were home from school for lunch.

The guide on my bus was a woman of about fifty or so and she was telling us that this island is known for three things, women, wind and storms. She said that females outnumber males on the island substantially as the men leave to find work. She also told us that the tradition in their culture was that females couldn't inherit and couldn't perform last-right ceremonies for their fathers, which is a big deal for her. When her father died she and her sister couldn't inherit his property so it passed to her male cousin who also did the last-rights. She was very upset about this even though a half-dozen years had passed. She was adamant that the cousin didn't give them what they felt was their due. They were even more upset about not being involved in the last-rights ceremony. Later we asked one of the male guides about this situation and he stated that was the old way of doing things which had changed in the past 50 years. It left us unsure about our guide's claims but the topic was heavy on her mind and heart—the poor thing.

One other item of interest on this island was the women who dive down to 100 feet according to our guide, searching for conical shells, abalone and other shellfish. She contended they use no equipment other then a weight belt and a hollowed out gourd filled with air allowing them to stay down in the water for up to thirty minutes. Again, we all wondered about these facts but some of the other guides told similar stories so it must be mostly true, I guess. People on one of the other buses said their guide's 70 year old mother was still actively diving; however, both guides said it is becoming a lost art because younger women prefer other ways to make money.

Our tour was finished ahead of schedule so our guide took us shopping at the same department store where Claudia's tour stopped; when I got off the bus I saw her waving at me. We met up and looked at all the over-priced stuff. She did buy a hat, a linen type of fabric that is dyed with local earth materials. This fabric is used for everything from hats to jackets and pants all had an earthy dull brown touch of pink color. Many of the women came back with those hats but I didn't see any other clothing items, maybe because everything looked the same and had the look of bad military khaki.

The island is volcanic ash turned to black top soil where most anything will grow. There are 13 cattle ranches in the steep areas with farms on the lower flat lands. They grow wheat and barley grains and tangerines plus a variety of other fruits and vegetables. There were several places where horse riding was available on the route my bus took. I asked why they didn't grow rice like the other areas; the guide said they couldn't raise rice because the pumice rock subsoil would not hold the water necessary for rice paddies.

Ancient Village school kids

Thatched roofed houses

CHAPTER 23

KAGOSHIMA, JAPAN

On this stop we took a tour to see the Chiran Samurai Houses and the Peace Museum which is dedicated to the Kamikaze Pilots of WWII.

The Samurai houses, more notably the gardens, have been in the Samurai families for 250 years — since the era when the Samurais ruled Japan. The homes are made of teakwood and have thatched roofs with sliding wooden doors that basically open much of the house to expose a veranda that nearly doubles the size of the living area. The veranda opens up to the beautiful and immaculately tended gardens including the green tea hedge that encircles many of the homes. The leaves are plucked yet today and are dried to make tea. Having grown up on a farm where you chew grain kernels to test their state of development, I tried chewing on some of these leaves but they didn't taste like much. The guide noticed me and laughed; she said that the flavor didn't come out until the leaves are dried. Then she imitated with her hands that you grind them up with your fingers and put them into your cup or tea pot. So much for the tea sampling — anyway we continued in this area, about a city block in size. Claudia asked how much these plots and houses cost? The guide indicated that they were very expensive, basically handed down from one generation to the next and that they couldn't be bought. When pressed she told Claudia they probably would cost 50 million Yen. They were extraordinarily beautiful, as only typical Japanese architecture and gardens can be.

The next stop was a museum they call the Peace Museum but it is a dedication to the kamikaze pilots of WWII. It is an exhibit that has several airplanes of the type used by those kids; most were 17 and 18 years old. Also displayed are their last wills and letters sent home to their mothers. The ones translated tell of a kid's pride in serving his country and how happy he was in his life at home, etc. It was a touching display and they point out, now, that war is useless. Interestingly they present their point of view about the war as a struggle to free the Pacific area from the impact of Western colonization. We were warned back in Darwin, Australia to expect such a point-of-view from the Japanese and they were correct. It is an interesting feature of humans to justify bad deeds, I remember one gangster from Al Capone's gang was quoted as saying that he didn't deserve to be in jail because he had only killed other "Punks", namely other gangsters.

There was a 30 minute presentation given by an older gentleman about these flyers. The planes were loaded with one 500 pound bomb and enough gasoline to get them one way. Their instructions were to fly into U.S. ships to make sure the bomb had maximum guidance to hit the ships. Bombs of that era that were dropped from airplanes stood a small chance of actually hitting their target. The one thing that surprised me, and most of us, was the fact there were only 1,039 of these flights; listening to our accounts of the war it seemed there were more. I do remember hearing a documentary on the history channel or some such place that the Japanese ran out of planes and fuel and everything else because we were bombing the mainland at this time and had sunk most of their navy, etc. I had one college friend whose father was on one of the ships. Claudia's cousin also was and the horror they tell about the war in general and the kamikazes specifically was beyond normal people's comprehension.

The presentation ended with an anti-war message that I thought really fell flat considering the Japanese reputation for cruelty towards prisoners of war and civilians in the areas they conquered. I remember the conversations with people in the Asian islands telling about the hell their fathers' generation went through when the Japanese controlled their lands. When the presentation was over one of the guys in our group stated they left one thing out and that was they locked the canopy of the airplanes once the kamikaze pilot got in so there was no escape for him by bailing out.

Shogun's gardens

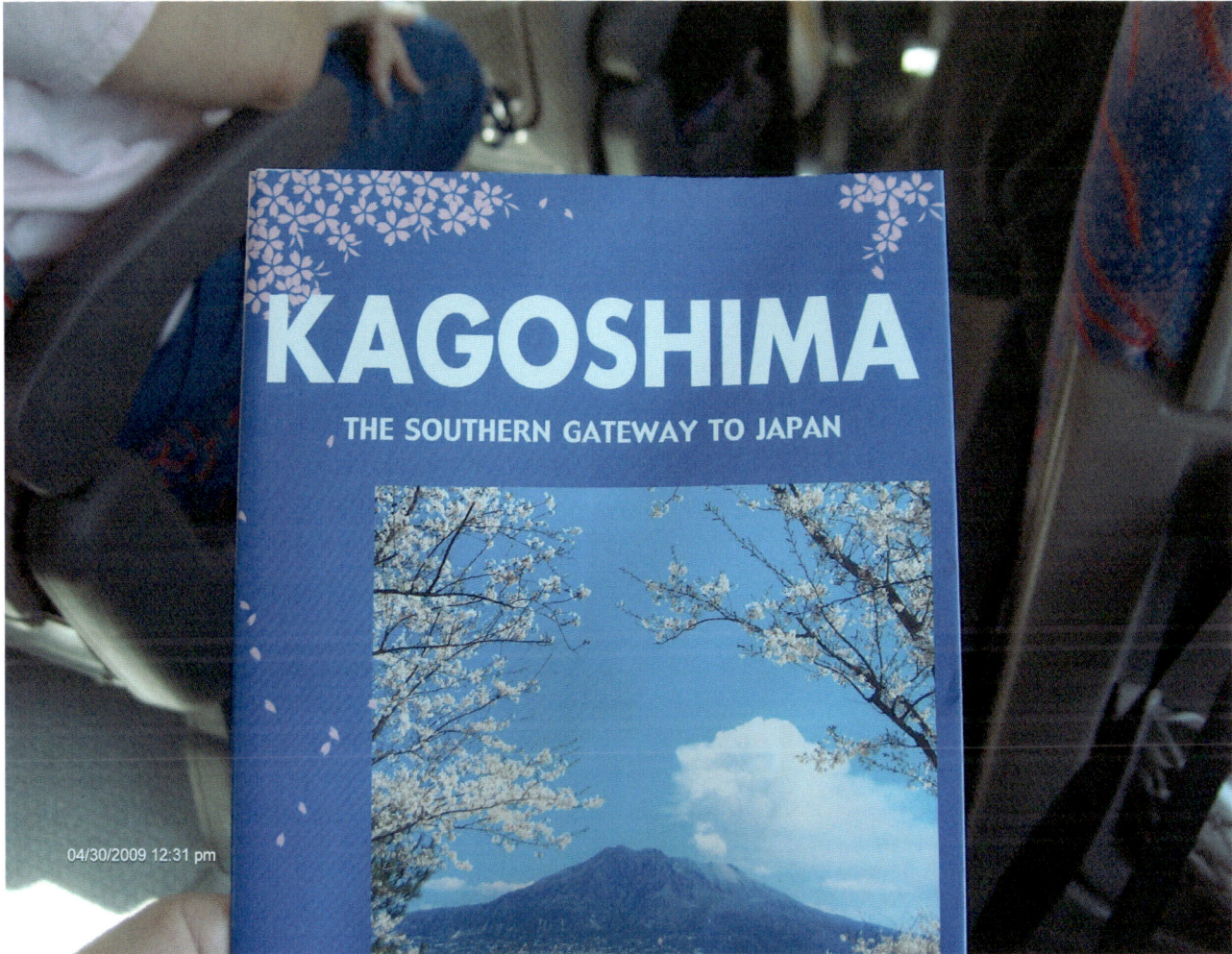

Japan First stop

Shogun's home

Shogun garden flowers and claudia

CHAPTER 24

KOBE, JAPAN

This city is sometimes called the Paris of Asia, so Claudia did what any red blooded American woman would do, she went shopping. There was a train that connected the ship terminal to the main railway station in the center of the city, so we took it that far and roamed around. We bought some T-shirts that we found were made in China when we got back to the ship. We experienced a situation the tour speaker told us about but we couldn't believe. That was if you had difficulty purchasing a ticket for the train you pushed a "help" button and a girl would pop out of the wall to help you. So when we did have difficulty with the ticket machine, I pushed the "help" button and sure enough, between two of the automatic ticketing machines in a space no more than 10 inches wide, a pretty young girl appeared. I was flabbergasted; I looked at her and looked at the little gap she stood in, sideways. She asked how many of us there were and where we were going, then she punched a couple of buttons and told us how much. I gave her the money which she put in the machine and out popped two tickets. It was incredible and I missed taking a picture of her because it all happened so fast. I needed a picture because nobody will ever believe there is a human small enough to fit into such a small space.

The area here is beautiful; the city is located along the water and backed up against a ridge of mountains which makes a gorgeous setting. The mountains are void of buildings except for a few homes that one would assume are very expensive.

The most interesting thing was, however, our stop into a Kimono shop because Claudia has been longing to get one. We looked at the cheap ones first, they cost about $100. Then we went to a real Kimono shop where we found out the good ones cost around $800 complete. A Kimono is a one-size fits all dress that wraps around a woman's body. The length is adjusted by folding the excess fabric around the waist and securing it with two pieces of ribbon; then the Obi, the traditional sash worn around the waist, is wrapped and tied with an extremely complex system of folding and knotting that leaves an elegant pouf in the back. After the demonstration of the Obi knotting system, it became obvious who would have to tie that, me, and that is something not easily learned. I was teasing an assistant that worked there, a young woman about twenty-two. I guessed that we would have to take her home with us to tie this thing up. Then she sheepishly revealed she didn't know how to do it either. Personally I don't even buy self-tie bow ties because my hands are not nimble enough to tie them. So we left without a Kimono and with an understanding of how complex the wrapping and obi tying would be if we ever got one. Still they were very beautiful, if impractical for a modern woman, Japanese or western.

We left the mall and went back out on the street where Claudia pointed out a Pachinko parlor that she insisted I experience. She had been in them before when she visited Japan. I took a picture to show how crowded they are. The game is a combination pinball machine and slot machine, it is loaded with little shiny silver colored balls that fall down through a series of pins like an old style pinball machine. Then they, or the player, somehow move things around to slow down or speed up the three rows of slot machine type of characters, stopping them where they hope for a line-up of symbols like a traditional slot machine. If the player wins, he is paid off in the little balls; some people had trays of them stacked up behind their chairs. The place was loud with the noise of the machines and the music; it was extremely smoky and filled to standing-room only. While we stood there, one young woman came and sat down with two trays of the silver balls and lost all of them in just a few minutes. The place is sort of a mini Las Vegas crammed into one small room.

I took some pictures of giggling, preteen girls; we met just walking down the street. In many cities the girls this age would say "Hello," as the met us and "Good bye" as they passed. We were told the kids here start to learn English in middle school, so the girls were testing their newly acquired language skills on us foreigners. I usually said, "Hello" which would make them turn around to look at me. Sometimes I would take their picture and they were always ready to pose; they would distort their bodies and hold up a "V" sign with their fingers. In one picture they had on school uniforms; but when they are on the streets they have T-shirts with English sayings, often risqué, inscribed on them. I doubt they or their parents have any idea what some of the sayings mean.

It is nearly midnight and we are about to shove off for Tokyo. There is a tug-boat just outside our window, waiting to help pull us away from the shore. These big ships don't usually need them but the first mate told us that the big ships have to hire them anyway; it keeps them in business. I could hear the tug on the radio with the bridge of our ship. Discussions went back and forth but the tug was never tied to our ship. We moved away under our own power. These new ships have propeller units front and back and each one pivots in a complete circle if needed, so the ship can move backwards, sideways angle-wise or any which way. Then, when the ship is moving forward it relies on two main propellers that turn at a constant rate and the propellers pitch can be changed like those on propeller airplanes to make the ship move at the desired speed.

As we move out through the harbor it always gives me a sinking feeling to look back and think about the apprehension I had when we first landed, wondering if we would find our way around without getting lost. Will we find the places we are interested in and if we will find things to purchase that we really want? Most of all is the concern of being able to get back to the ship before it leaves, not a small concern in many places where you don't speak the language and rush hour traffic can tie up the taxis or other transportation systems. That is one of the huge benefits of going with a group on a tour; you know the ship won't leave without a group of you. However, it does happen that somebody doesn't get back to the ship on time and they get left; I have heard of it more than once. Sometimes a tug boat will take them on and speed out to catch the ship or the pilot boat will pick them up and transfer the passenger when the pilot gets off a few miles from shore. Sometimes passengers have to travel overland or fly to the next port to catch up.

Now as we move further away from the port I look back and think of how we did find our way around with no trouble and remembering the great food we found on our own, even though we don't speak a word of Japanese.

It's one of the things I experienced when working on audits, you go to a new place, learn about everything they do, make new friends and business acquaintances. Then in a couple of weeks you finish and leave knowing there is little chance you will ever go back and/or meet those people again. Then you have to move on to new assignments and challenges, like it or not and the whole process goes on again. It's like kissing a girl you really like for the first time and go away knowing you will never see her again.

It's a beautiful night to sail and as we move further away from the port, the air is fresh and crisp and the lights of the city shimmer off the water. The ship slips stealthily through the night like it's hiding the fact it is taking us away from a place we barely got to know and like. The ship seems to know it's doing wrong, so uses darkness and the time we sleep to ease the sense of loss for us.

Japanese vending machines

04/30/2009 5:59 pm

Japanese Middle School girls

Japanese Pachinko parlor

English practicing girls

CHAPTER 25

TOKYO, JAPAN

I sat this one out with a cold and a cough that couldn't be managed on a bus full of people, so Claudia and I went to sick bay and the doc gave my some antibiotics to kill the sore throat. He mentioned he didn't think it was strep throat but he wanted to be safe. I have never had that but have known people, mostly college kids, that have had it and it's hard to get rid of. He did mention that there was a virus on board that just has to work itself out. I got some cough medicine and an inhaler; anyway the program worked and in a few days I was ready to go again.

Claudia went on the tour which covered some of the city and included a walk in the Imperial Palace Gardens which she felt was a disappointment. It was not as beautifully planted as some other places she had been. She has been in Japan many times before. Sarah, her daughter, taught English in Japan for some years. In Japan she had come to expect spectacular gardens whereas these were just grand. Her bus got caught in traffic on the way home...they were late, which concerned me mightily. While shopping she got her eyes made up by some porcelain skinned women who had some eye liner that did make her look good and she was very proud of it. The tour she was on provided lunch which she said was too westernized when compared to so many wonderful meals we had found ourselves at different stops on the trip.

I joined our table for dinner the second night ending my self-imposed quarantine. It was good to get back to normal even if the food I selected wasn't so hot. I had spent the day watching old movies and whatever was on the TV, plus I rented a DVD, "Chicago." I love musicals and Claudia doesn't like to watch them over and over as much as I do, so I watch them when she is elsewhere. I pick out the dance routines I like and skip much of the rest.

At 9:00 pm we shoved off from Tokyo headed north up the coast of Japan to the next port of call; we have only two stops left before we cross the North Pacific to Alaska. The harbor is long here and we have spent more than an hour sailing out of it and the captain has got his foot on the gas. We are moving right along for being in a fairly congested harbor.

Once out of the harbor there were lights of the settlements along the shore as far as the eye could see. It's always interesting to look at those lights and imagine what is going on in those houses. When I was going to college I went home to my family's farm on most weekends to work. Between the farm and grain elevator Dad ran, there was always much to do. I often got assigned work in the elevator as my three younger brothers were able to do much of the farm work. At the elevator, amongst other things, I would unload a box-car load of coal and deliver it to the town Court House, the school and the library. That was hard work; I had to shovel off the first quarter of the car with a regular grain shovel and pitch it into a truck. Then, once there was some working room in the boxcar, I used a huge shovel with two small rubber wheels under it. This worked by going as fast as you could, scraping the shovel along the floor of the boxcar and jamming it as hard as you can into the coal. This would load the shovel then you would push down on the handles and wheel the shovel full of coal over into the truck and dump it. Once the truck was loaded, I drove it to the point of delivery and raised the hoist to dump the truck-load of coal into the basement of the building. My other tasks at the elevator were to truck feed and grain to and from various places; since I was the eldest of four brothers these trucking tasks fell to me. Of course, when the weather was bad I would stay at school but my education money came from working and there was always plenty of work. Anyway when I drove back to Grand Forks from Kathryn, North Dakota it would be late Sunday night and I always admired the people I could see snug in their homes…I was always a little jealous of them. I hoped some day I would be able to spend my Sunday nights at home. Then when I went to work for the two multi-national corporations for twenty years, I again had to travel on Sunday nights. I always hated being in an airport watching part of a sports game while waiting for the next flight. All throughout those years I traveled about half the time, many Sunday nights. Of course, I always had good company as many other men also traveled for their jobs. The airline pilots, most of the time, would apprise us passengers of the scores or at least the final score of the game of the night. Since I retired I don't have to be gone on Sunday nights any more and I am thankful for that.

Claudia mentioned to me before we went to dinner that it is incredible to remember that we were at war with Japan and bombed the city of Tokyo to the ground. The allies of WWII learned while bombing German cities that if they bombed in two rings about a mile apart, the two fires swept towards each other creating a fire storm. This kind of bombing was devastating and that is what Tokyo was subjected to in early 1945. What made the bombing so horrific was the fact the buildings were nearly all made of wood, so they burned hot and fast. Now as I look out across the city it seems like such a waste — which war really is — but men will be men and some just can't wait to send thousands to their deaths.

CHAPTER 26

HAKODATE, JAPAN

A trip to the city on a shuttle bus proved to be a good day for Claudia. We went to the fish market and found a place that cooks fresh crab Japanese-style. It was prepared part tempera style, part as sushi, and part cooked; it was very good. We, especially Claudia, loves crab. Then we were on our way into a store when we ran into another couple from the ship and the woman told us how she found used kimonos a few miles across the city. They showed us the trolley to take to get there, so even though we didn't have much time, we got there, bought a used kimono and made it back to the shuttle on time. There were anxious moments on the trolley; the map we had didn't show the current routes. But, but trolley operator was very helpful, even though she didn't speak very much English. Since this was one of our last stops in Japan we had given up on getting a kimono, so Claudia was thrilled with our find and it made the trip to this port memorable.

Our lunch

Hakodate Japan fish market Squid

CHAPTER 27

OTARU, JAPAN

In Otaru we docked by a group of steel Quonsets that are used to store ships' supplies as we found out when we were walking into town. They were moving huge bags of rice onto the ship for our kitchens. Looking into the buildings I could see other food-stuffs and supplies, but I couldn't identify some of the storehouse items. However, the building inside was immaculate, so I assume that much of what was stored there was for human consumption such as flour, salt and grains of various kinds.

It was interesting to note that a ship, in at the end of the pier, was being loaded by longshoremen. That was of note because most things today are shipped by container. In earlier days a huge group of men called longshoremen loaded things by pallets using a series of nets and cranes, a labor intensive and slow procedure. There were more opportunities to damage goods with that system; there is a lot of protection afforded by a steel box that can be carefully packed. Of course, containers are hard to inspect, a problem for security people working the piers.

For those who are not familiar with the container method of shipping, a container is a steel box are about 25 feet long and 8 feet high and wide where one end opens up completely. A shipper, say of furniture, rents this box and loads it, packing each piece carefully. The container is then loaded on a flat bed truck and hauled to the port. Here the containers are kept until a ship-load is assembled. Then huge cranes stack them up on the top of a ship designed to handle them and once at the destination port the process is reversed.

We had a nice walk into town, about six blocks from the ship. We saw a KFC restaurant, a sign of America. We also encountered a covered street made into a mall of sorts. We shopped our way down this street until we got hungry, so we started back and found a nice restaurant. The sign in front had the menu in English so we went in to find out about it but no one inside understood a word of English. We ordered the two lunch specials and both turned out to be delicious; one was a noodle soup dish, the other was rice with pork. We still don't know why the rice in Asia is so tasty; one thing we have noticed is that the soy sauce they use is much sweeter and thicker than ours, almost like molasses but even without this, the rice tastes so much better. We don't know why but are on the quest to find out.

This city along the water is like the others, seemingly quite progressive and clean. As one of the speakers we have had on board asked, "Have you seen a dirty car?" It's a trick question because there aren't any dirty cars. One wonders how they all afford to live, as there doesn't seem to be much industry but they seem quite well-off. We haven't seen any area that looks like a poor section or a run-down area. Maybe if such an area exists it must be back in the hills somewhere. This port was very tourist-oriented; when the ship was leaving they had the same drum corps that welcomed us and a couple of dozen people with flags waved good bye to us. Cruise ships no doubt constitute a lot of business for them. Hundreds of people from our ship were walking around town; in addition, there were others who must be people that came to shop via land or air, as we observed many other non-Japanese people in town that were not from our ship.

We also stopped at an ice cream shop and had a dish of ice cream. I took a picture of the sign and how they spelled "dairy farm" as "daily farm;" the woman running the place also posed for our camera.

05/07/2009 1:43 pm

Otaru Japan

05/07/2009 1:45 pm

Rice and flour for our ship

05/07/2009 4:39 pm

The Volendam

Otaru City canel

YAMANAKA
DAILY FARM

ミルク

ソフトクリーム

ショップ

05/07/2009 4:20 pm

Ice Cream shop

The ice cream girl

CHAPTER 28

AOMORI, JAPAN

This is the last shore excursion of our Asian trip. Tonight we head for Alaska and home, even though Claudia threatens to stay on the ship.

Today's tour was the last in Asia, but probably the best. We had the best bus tour-guide of the lot; she was easy to understand, funny, extremely informative and pleasant. Getting up in her twenties, she is or will soon become, a "Christmas Cake." That is what the Japanese call an unmarried women over 25; what we refer to as an "Old Maid." However, in the new world of people marrying later in life, I doubt this means much. Anyway she started off the tour by announcing she was in need of a boyfriend and asked for volunteers. With this age group and every man here with his spouse (most for many years) or another woman, understandably no guys raised their hands. Her approach was maybe a little corny but she immediately showed her warmth and sense of humor and from that point on, she had us all eating out of the palm of her hand. This girl is way too good for this job; she should be running for political office or something. If I knew I could get her to manage my campaign, I would move here and run for office myself; the other poor guys wouldn't have a chance.

We moved away from the ship, through town in the fog, and for an hour and a half we meandered our way up-hill, a long way up-hill, and far into the countryside. Within two hours the fog lifted to reveal miles and miles of cherry and apple trees in full-bloom on either side of the road; we hit the peak of blossom time! Many on the cruise were afraid we would be too late in the season but because of the cold spring, the blossoms were some weeks late. The blossoms hung in clumps and Claudia said, "I have never seen anything like it... unforgettable beauty."

I have to say that we had incredibly great weather throughout the entire trip. On the days we spent touring, the weather was almost perfect, not once did we get rained on. The tropics were hot but that is expected and we only had two or three days when the sea was moderately rough.

Our first stop on this island was at an ancient temple, a beautiful castle of some grand Shogun. The place was up-hill and with a very steep stairs inside. We only went on the first floor because we are not good at stairs. Inside one item of interest was a Shogun's suit of protective clothing made from tightly woven fabric. It may have given as much protection as a metal suit of armor because some of the new bullet proof vests use fabrics that are more effective than metal and much lighter and cooler. There was also a carrier used to move the Shogun around; it was a three foot cube with a long pole on top that several men, front and back, carried on their shoulders. The person inside the carriage would sit with his legs crossed as they do when they eat; even with this method of sitting, the person inside must have been relatively short because of the small space.

After we left the castle we looked at a Festivity Hall where items are stored that make up big floats for parades they have throughout the year. They had a shop in the back that made things like children's toy tops and other wood-formed items. Claudia bought a red ball an inch around on a rope necklace; it is made from lacquer paint layered in multiple coats.

From here we had lunch at a nice place but the food was marginal. Then we went to an area where there were many Buddhist temples where the ashes of the deceased are buried or incased in an enclosure of some kind. The interesting part of these temples is that they are also houses where the monks live with their families. The monks are wealthy men and they build these fancy temples/houses, and because they are designated official Buddhist Temples, people can bury their kin here. The families of the deceased have to pay a yearly fee to the temple for this right.

We had the final stop at another temple, a five story building used for prayer. A giant bell was located in the courtyard under a roof. A log on two chains swung so it could ram the bell that made the deep bonging sound associated with Buddhist bells. You were supposed to make a small monetary contribution to ring the bell…we all had to ring the bell. At this temple there was a wall with wooden shingles about eighteen inches long and four inches wide that contained a donor's name and the amount of money each family gave to store their ancestor's ashes here. This system was also used at the other temples. Our guide told us that the Japanese people were very competitive and gave lots of money to protect their status with the living and with the gods.

Rice planting time

Aomori mountian

05/08/2009 1:14 pm

Aomori Cherry blossoms

Shogun Castle

hanging cherry blosoms & Claudia

Art on the dock

05/08/2009 8:06 pm

Aomori Bridge

CHAPTER 29
A SUMMARY OF THE TIGERS

Japan concludes our visit to the tiger economies. As we sail out into the Northern Pacific, we have time to reflect on what we have observed. Claudia who was in China in 1979 says, "The changes are beyond my wildest imagination. In those days everyone wore Mao suits and rode bicycles; now they are dressed western style and are "Hip" moving at a pace that's hard to believe. In 1979 we could only get ice for drinks where each cube was wrapped individually in paper and rationed very closely. Now the hotels and business are the same as anywhere in the west."

If we contemplate what we have observed, it would center on the industriousness of the people. They are, in our opinion, where the U.S. was, in say 1950, where at gas stations two guys would run out to pump gas in your car while washing the windows and checking the air in the tires. They have a huge labor pool eager to work and it's hard to see how we in the west are going to compete, save a few technology enhancements or breakthroughs. The people of the South Pacific live on peanuts compared to the U.S., Europe or Japan. In China the wages are comparatively low so it seems to us that what has been happening in China, gaining manufacturing in the last decades, will continue.

The past year has seen China shutting down factories because of low export demand. It is certainly true that they manufactured to feed the West's consumption bubble of the past decades but now that's mostly over. We in the West have spent our inheritance and all the money we could borrow and are trillions of dollars in debt to the saving conscious Chinese. Individuals that still have jobs in the consuming countries have become thriftier caused by the fear of worse economic times ahead. In any event the slow down in US consumption has caused a drop in the need of items produced by China and to some degree the other tiger economies.

Strangely, on our trip it was not evident that the recession has had much of an effect in this area of the world. Things looked progressive, busy and no one (namely local tour-guides) said anything about the downturn. I quizzed several of them and the response was something like, "Well I heard about somebody that lost their job but no one close to me."

I never know how to evaluate those kinds of answers and the national statistics, propaganda, put out by the country are probably not much better than my little poll.

One of the most notable things about these countries is the people's dress. They dress western style and look better than most people on the streets in the U.S. Everyone we saw, with the exception of a rare beggar, looked well dressed and clean. We never saw any of the super baggy pants hanging half way off their butts like many kids in the U.S.

A practice one of the ladies at our dinner table observed was the closeness of girlfriends. They hold hands as they walk and they walk very close together; she thought that was a good sign for girls to have best friends forever, (BFF) I guess is the popular acronym for it. Having four daughters between Claudia and me, we don't remember seeing quite that level of affection with our girls and their friends.

I didn't do any research to confirm or deny the fact that I feel these cultures have nuclear families where there is a father in the household. But this is evident by observing that women are shopping with their kids in the middle of a week day — Dad is at work and Mom stays home with the kids and on weekends the whole family goes shopping.

Discipline and respect for elders is very strong in these cultures. They worship and continue to pay for a resting place for the ashes of the dearly departed forever and as a guide in Japan told us, "We are very vain and don't want others to look down on us. So we pay good money to the temple that stores the ashes of the departed to keep up appearances and outdo one another."

I think my reflection of the trip turns back to kids. I can't get them out of my mind; they are so clean, well dressed and polite. These kids are like we were in the 1950's when I was a kid. My generation was subjected to the pressure of the Sputnik Syndrome and I think these kids are in a similar situation. When I started college in 1960 and if you were male you had to go into the sciences or become an engineer; otherwise you were a commie pinko—a traitor to your country. Catching up to the Russians was our obligation — our responsibility — the country was in our hands. Worse — the preceding generation fought and died keeping the country safe from Fascism — we had the challenge to keep it safe from Communism.

The issue for the young people of Asia, in my opinion, is the idea that they can do anything that we can do, if they get educated. Our invincibility image was lost when we pulled out of Vietnam and when the Japanese went from a defeated, destroyed nation to one that out-performed the great U.S. economy in the 1980's. They even bought U.S. showcase properties like the Pebble Beach Golf Course and landmark buildings in New York City ... of course that bubble has now burst. The only advantage the U.S. now holds is a thin lead in technology areas. The young of the world are being preached to that technology and knowledge is their ticket out of poverty and their generation carries the responsibility to lead their people upward—no pressure.

Technology is a moving target and there are areas of inventiveness that takes a level of sophistication that many countries don't have, so these are the areas that we must focus on. The other issue is energy replacement which is a sore point with me. We have the ability to produce more then twenty percent of the energy we need from bio-fuel namely ethanol produced from corn. Corn is a renewable resource; a new crop grows every year. This product is in trouble because of the price of feed stock, gasoline prices and because of oil company propaganda against it.

CHAPTER 30

CRUISING ACROSS THE NORTH PACIFIC OCEAN

We enjoyed a few days of welcome rest at sea. It seems like an oxymoron to be tired while on vacation. However, landing at a different port each day almost requires one to go sightseeing; otherwise you might miss something important. Besides you can't very well say you were some place, but don't know anything about it; besides most ports-of-call are interesting. So now it is rest and relaxation and collecting our thoughts about what we have seen and to take a little time to work on putting pictures together with written material; much of it is a matter of culling out the bad pictures.

The days at sea heading towards Alaska are a time for us to enjoy the two speakers on board, a naturalist and an historian. The naturalist is a photographer of some repute who talks about sea mammals, whales, sea lions, harbor seals, porpoises and birds. The other guy talks about the history of Europeans exploring the area, namely Bering a Danish/Russian adventurer sent by Czar Peter the Great to explore "his country" and find Alaska.

It took Vitus Bering, and his force of hundreds, three years to go overland and get to the Pacific Ocean by crossing Siberia. They built two ships and sailed into horrific storms common in the Northern Pacific; he lost his second ship before finding Alaska. When they found Alaska they stayed for only One Day—after all the time they spent getting there! On the return trip, his ship the St. Peter ran aground on an island about one hundred miles from the shores of Russia. Here, due to the stress of the grueling past four years, plus his age and obesity, he died. The island was later named for him and a monument was erected in his honor. His crew carried Bering's story back to Russia but by that time Czar Peter had died and all interest in the expedition was lost. Only the efforts of a handful of people carried his legacy forward in the decades that followed.

CHAPTER 31

KODIAK, ALASKA

I knew we were docking by the noises the ship was making and by looking at the clock; I could tell it was time to be in port. It was early morning but I stumbled out on the veranda and I could barely see the water by looking straight down the fog was so thick—and that's foggy. Life on ship continued in spite of the fog; the U.S. immigration and custom authorities came on board and once again we all had to line up and show our passports and get them stamped. We also handed in a customs declaration card but they did nothing with it. We docked about seven a.m. and it was nine-thirty by the time Claudia and I were able to get on land and look for our tour.

I thought the tours might be called off but everything moved forward. The fog started to burn off and you could see about a half mile but the ceiling was just a few hundred feet. Everyone else on the tours ahead of ours moved on land without hesitation and we followed. We went to find our bus and were a little surprised to see they were using school buses. The bus driver, tour-guide/cheerleader shooed us on the bus declaring, "Oh, it will clear up soon." She gleefully took us through her "city" jabbering all the while. Her city was only a series of sparsely placed stores along the highway. There were a couple of fish processing plants along the shore and the largest Coast Guard facility in the nation, according to her.

She drove us around for an hour and then she could tell the fog had lifted more inland so she took us to the only golf course on the island. It was a nine hole course but it looked like it was used as more of a driving range. When we got there the sky was nearly clear and we could see the mountains which were quite majestic. One had a mountain goat, the city mascot, sitting on a high perch apparently his favorite place. Once we got back to town the fog had lifted so we could see more of the little town that was twisted around the valley between the mountains

This was our first stop in Alaska and it was not disappointing. The rugged wilderness was a huge contrast to the flat rice paddy lands of Asia where we had been for the past two months. Kodiak is very rural, small town U.S.A., the northern version, where life goes on at a slower pace.

A huge tsunami caused by an earthquake hit Alaska in 1963 which destroyed their original cannery. So they found an old liberty ship pulled it in and used it to quickly re-establish the business. It has now been incorporated into the permanent operation. Maybe it is part of a contingency plan in case of flood waters again. During WWII when Hitler sunk one ship every day we built one every day. When I worked for

Combustion Engineering they had a foundry in Chattanooga, Tennessee. When our audit team was there the chief financial officer told us that during WWII they turned out one boiler for a ship every day, therefore the war years were their best years.

Our affable driver would have showed us more, but by that time we had taken more than two hours for a one hour scheduled trip. Someone on her radio was questioning where she was so she took us back to the ship. However, she admitted she didn't have anything to do until she had to take the school kids home that afternoon.

05/15/2009 5:31 am

Kodiak fish processing plant

largest Coast Guard base

Kodiak golf course

CHAPTER 32

HOMER, ALASKA

This town is smaller than Kodiak; here we had a ticket to ride a shuttle around town that delivered the ship's passengers to five different drop-off points. It was cold, windy and misty or raining much of the time. The visibility was good in the early morning but deteriorated all day long. We were late to get on the shuttle and when we got on the bus there were only four of us. However, as we got to the other pickup points, all the people who had gotten an early start were now ready to come back and the buses were full and struggling to keep up. Worse, it started to rain and few people were equipped for that. We stayed on the bus and made the loop around the city and came directly back to the ship. This was to avoid being left out in the rain like all the rest of the poor souls trying to get on a shuttle. One of the port authorities had informed, Claudia, who always asks everybody she sees about a good place to eat, found out that a restaurant close to the ship was recommended. We tried it out and they had the best king crab either of us had ever eaten. It was "heavenly", according to Claudia and this went a long way toward honing her opinion of Alaska.

Homer watering hole

People camping

CHAPTER 33

SITKA, ALASKA

We had to use the life boats to get to the port so the ship could stay anchored in the deeper water. Here we didn't go to the ship's theater where we usually went to get group assignment numbers; on this tour we were responsible to get to our own bus at the assigned time.

We first went to a Totem Pole Museum and a nature walk. We spent half an hour at the gift shop of the museum before driving to a hospital for crippled Bald Eagles called the Raptor Center. This was a very interesting institution, a non-profit that sustains itself with memberships and donations. They bring in enough money to sustain several buildings with large outside cages, a veterinary surgery room and a staff of about a dozen. Injured eagles are brought here and are patched up or put to sleep. They had about a dozen birds there in various stages of healing. Their main objective is to fix the birds so they can be returned to the wild, however, they told us some are injured to the point they cannot be released. We saw a female that is just such a bird and is used for demonstration purposes and to educate the public about eagles. The handlers even take them on trips around the country and find homes for the crippled birds in zoos. They showed us one that was very even-tempered and didn't even mind flash cameras which I thought was incredible. We spent an hour and a half at this place and bought some T-shirts that have a picture of a big stern looking eagle with a caption that states, "I Am Smiling." I wore it at home in Houston on Halloween, much to the delight of the trick-or-treat kids.

The next stop was to watch a group of women dancers perform traditional Russian routines in honor of the two hundred years of Russian control of this area. The Russians sold Alaska to the U.S. in 1913 for seven million dollars. During WWII the largest construction job of the war was the building of a road to Alaska from the mainland. This was done because of the fear the Japanese would invade Alaska and an overland route was needed to move men and supplies. The Japanese did, in fact, invade two of the Aleutian Islands, which were held for some time. One was taken back with the loss of a few thousand American soldiers. The second island had causalities of 300 who were tragically killed by friendly fire before it was discovered that the Japanese had abandoned the island.

After the dancers performed, we visited an interesting Russian Orthodox Church in the middle of town. The tour was over and we spent the next two hours shopping. We found a good restaurant and had King Crab again; it was wonderful. Before long it was time to go back to the ship for a 6 o'clock sail away and we loaded up in one of the tenders and got back on board. The day was like the other two we had spent on shore here in Alaska; it was cloudy and rainy. The people said that here in Sitka they get a 1/3 of an inch of rain every day. It is considered a "temperate-rain-forest" according to one of the guides. The scenery was spectacular as was the food.

Sitka Alaska

injured Eagle center

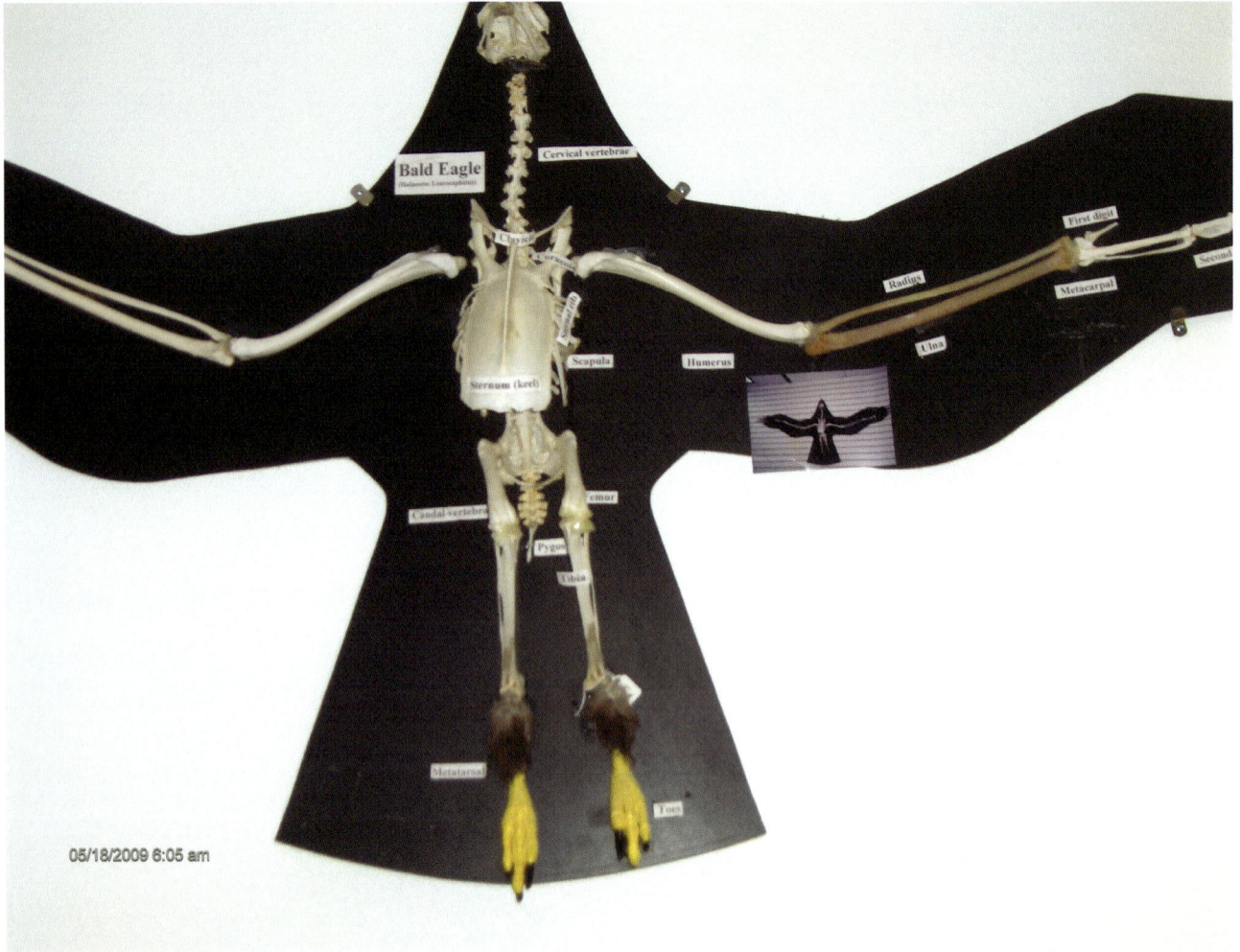

Eagle skeleton

Folk dancers

CHAPTER 34

KETCHIKAN, ALASKA

At this port our ship was not the only one in port; there were two other passenger ships at the dock along with us. There was a Norwegian Line ship that was nearly twice the size of our ship and a Princess Line ship that was about the same size as ours. This put a lot of people in the shops of this little town but they seemed to be geared up for it. The shops where we purchased things had plenty of cashiers and the sales staffs were very efficient.

We took a boat tour to the Misty Fjords where we saw wonderful landscapes but not very many sea creatures, some eagles and an eagle's nest. The boat was comfortable, had nice facilities such as diet coke for sale in the galley and nice seating; everything we needed for a pleasant trip.

I took a lot of pictures of the mountains, the trees, the eagle's nest and rock formations. The tour boat crew passed around some bite sized strudels in the morning and clam chowder at noon; both were excellent. We got back to the port about 1 o'clock, which left us three hours to look around the town. There we bought some gifts and a few necessities at a drug store. It was a cruise-ship paradise in that the little town was filled with tourist-trap shops right across the street from the harbor. About half of those businesses were jewelry stores but the other half were well stocked with gift items, clothing and Alaskan souvenirs. Here the merchants only sell articles that are made in Alaska.

05/19/2009 2:53 am

Ketchacan Alaska

05/19/2009 2:57 am

Coast guard gun boat

Going to see a fjord

a fjord

05/19/2009 12:38 pm

our ship

CHAPTER 35

THE PEOPLE WE MET ON THE SHIP

As I look back on this and other cruises the memories that stay with me are those of the people we have met. The ones you become most familiar with, of course, are the people that sit at your dinner table. You gather together with them each night and discuss the events of the day…much as many families do around the evening meal. On this trip we asked to be seated at a table for six. On the first part of the journey, before Hong Kong, we sat with four ladies from Australia. Then on the remaining leg of the trip, we joined a table where Paul and Ellen were sitting and then we were joined by Stan from New York and Lori from New Zealand.

The Australian ladies

Our table mates for the first twenty days of the trip were four ladies from Australia…we really enjoyed their company and learned a lot about Australia too. They were with us while we sailed around the east and northeast parts of the country and they filled us in on these areas as we toured and sailed around them.

Paul and Ellen

Paul and Ellen were the only other couple at our table; he was and is still a veterinary Professor who for many years worked at the Agricultural University in Fargo, North Dakota. When I was still working on our family farm in North Dakota, I occasionally took sick animals to their veterinary clinic for a post-mortem diagnosis. Paul worked in that department and likely worked on some of the animals I brought in. I don't have any independent recollection of him; but that was forty years ago and who worked there was not the focus of my trips. Paul and Ellen moved many years ago to the University of Georgia in Athens. I had an audit assignment in that city when I worked for ABB; they bought the Westinghouse transformer division which included a manufacturing plant in Athens. It is an interesting and physically beautiful place with an equally interesting history. The local plant manager took the other auditor and me on a tour of the city. The highlight was the huge number of antebellum homes. He told us the reason Sherman on his march across Georgia in the Civil War, didn't burn Athens was because his roommate at West Point was from there, and so he spared the city. Paul and Ellen are very well traveled and have cruised many places. They, like we, have been on many different cruise lines and frequent cruisers love to discuss our impressions of the various companies. We enjoyed their company very much.

Stan

Stan, our table-mate from New York, is a retired teacher. He was alone. A pleasant and talkative fellow, he was a pleasure at the table and Claudia and I occasionally ran across him in the Crow's Nest bar; he was always sitting alone.

The Crow's Nest bar is located on the top level of the ship facing forward; it is a place where sail-away parties and special events are held. At night either the ship's band played, as for the "Balls" they had, or a disc jockey played songs from the era of the nightly designated theme. Sadly the DJ always played everything too loud which drove us and most people out. People our age want to talk and be in a quieter environment.

Lori

Lori, our other table-mate, joined us at Hong Kong. She is a Kiwi, a person from New Zealand. She is also a retired teacher and Dean of Students at a women's high school. She is single and always was, as far as we could tell. She was the conundrum of the group to me. She was friendly, easy spoken and flirtatious with men; for her to never have had a steady man in her life is hard for me to believe. She was fiercely independent and could walk faster then any human I ever knew; on land tours she would walk all over the cities we visited. Most of us were lucky to see one area. She has traveled the world many times…a really neat lady.

Blanch

Blanche is one of the women on the trip that lived alone in an expensive cabin, meaning she must have money. She reminds me of the song "Copacabana" sung by Berry Manilow and goes like this, "Her name was Lola, she was a show girl, with a yellow feather in her hair and a dress cut down to there." The story continues that, "Tony always tended bar, they were young and had each other." When a rich man, Rico, makes moves on Lola, "But Rico went a bit too far, Tony sailed across the bar. There was a gun shot and Lola lost her love. That was thirty years ago when they had a show, now it's a disco, but not to Lola. She sits there faded feather in her hair and drinks herself half blind. She lost her youth and lost her Tony, now she lost her mind.

Blanche, once the beauty of wherever she lived, now appears in twenty-year old fashions with back combed hair puffed up on her head like a bird nest. Desperately lonely, she tries to attach herself to anyone that doesn't run away from her. Decked out in expensive jewelry and still buying more, including a $25,000 necklace she bought on the ship. She often speaks of a husband who she says might join her at the end of the cruise. He didn't and I suspect never does. I think he is an ex or someone who ignores her and probably has a girlfriend. I base this mostly on a conversation I once had with her when she lost a credit card and didn't know how she was going to contact the company to cancel the card. I asked her if she couldn't contact her husband at which she barked in a muffled tone, "He doesn't have anything to do with my stuff!" She was ditsy without question but I felt sorry for her. If she was my mother, I would wish people would treat her nicely in spite of her flaws. We did some things with her and she was fun sometimes.

Our table mates

Ships librarian

ship towel art

CHAPTER 36

VANCOUVER, CANADA

The day finally came that we had to leave the ship. All day long I felt that we needed to get back to the ship before it sailed that night.

Claudia's angst was that, "Someone else will be in room 7066 tonight, our room, how dare they give our little cabin to someone else!"

No more dinners with the usual table mates and no more five course meals with tea after. No more rush to get to the auditorium for the nightly show followed by the daily corny joke of the cruise director. She was a sweet, pretty lady, but a terrible joke teller. It has always puzzled me but female comedians are few and far between. Maybe nobody can think of their sweet loving mother, wife or sister as a jokester. I guess it is the bawdy-bold male image that's needed to tell jokes which are usually a little risqué. This would not be lady-like and might tarnish a woman's image with other women. There's always an exception and Tina Fey is one. When she impersonates Sarah Palin she is hilarious and I can never tell them apart when they are on TV. Worse is when the real Sarah comes on and talks her stupid dribble wearing clothes that vary from fit for a slut to that of a scrub woman, she makes me laugh.

We landed on Wednesday May 22, 2009; getting off the ship went smoothly even with all our 20 bags. We were fortunate in finding a man with a big cart that loaded up all of them. Then a kindly customs lady took our declarations card and made a mark on it and we just moved right through the area to a cab. Lucky for us the next cab in the lineup was a minivan so the driver was able to get everything in. We went to the Sutton Place Hotel in downtown Vancouver and in minutes we were in our suite with a kitchen, living room and bedroom, it was very spacious and welcome after being crammed in the ship's cabin for two months. We were looking for a reason to be gone from "our ship" and this room helped.

Next we took a tour of the city for about four hours. Vancouver is a beautiful place. We were supposed to fly home the next day, but we had the concierge check the cost of flying back with so much luggage and found out it would be close to three grand and even shipping it back was about the same price. Thus, we decided to drive back and spend that money on renting a car; great logic, anything to extend the trip and put off going back to Houston in the heat of the summer

The next day we took another tour to Victoria, Canada which entailed a three hour drive and a two hour ferry ride. It was a full day with only four hours left to look at an absolutely beautiful botanical garden that was created in an abandoned surface mine. Victoria is the provincial capitol of British Columbia and considers itself the most "British" of all the cities in Canada. The picturesque architecture, an elegant Victorian and Edwardian-era design, includes stately hotels, mansions and government buildings. Victoria has masqueraded as 19th century London or Paris on the silver screen.

Claudia was disappointed in one thing and that was the lack of the street lamps with hanging flower baskets that we saw in an advertisement. There were many beautiful, expensive homes along the numerous water-front areas because the city is built on land that has a series of inlets from the ocean.

Next we took a day off! We were tired from all the touring and traveling and it felt good to just stay in the room and go across the street for a nice dinner.

The following day we went to Whistler, a ski resort where the Winter Olympics will be held in the spring of 2010. It was a beautiful drive up to the resort. Once there, we took an airplane ride to look at the glaciers. I felt we got gypped out of viewing the glaciers from the cruise ship when we were in Alaska. The advertisement about the trip explained we would sail up to the glaciers but it didn't happen. As with other schedule changes on this cruise, the ship's captain gave no reason. The airplane ride was magnificent, flying over the mountain peaks and looking down at the massive formations was great. The thing I didn't realize was that there are huge crevices existing in the ice. I have always heard that adventurers fall into these deep cracks in the glacier, but until you actually look down into them, do you realize their immensity and depth. Back on the ground we looked at the preparations going on for the events in the spring and knew we could now watch the Olympics with knowledge of the area.

We took the next day to repack our luggage. Then, because we weren't going directly home, we needed to find a dentist to fix Claudia's tooth that had lost its filling during the cruise.

We then took a bus to Seattle to rent an SUV to drive home with all our booty. We had quite a time with the US customs officials at the border. I don't think they had ever encountered anyone with that much luggage and they held us there with dogs sniffing our 20 bags until they figured out what to do. The rest of the three dozen people on the bus had, at most, two small bags and were becoming upset with the delay we were causing. It was clear the man who was in charge had trouble with such a decision and held several conferences with the other agents until they finally told us to go through.

We had never visited Washington State and so we spent two days in Seattle before going to Mt. Rainer where we stayed two days at a ski lodge.

Claudia has a high school friend and her husband who live in Newport, Oregon. She has invited Claudia to come and visit her for years so we spent several very pleasant days with them.

Then, Claudia's sister, Carol, lives in Carmel, California, only 600 miles south, right down the road, a stones throw considering the miles we have traveled in the past two months. The road to Carmel took us through the spectacular Redwood Forest and Ukiah, California where Claudia went to high school. We spent the night there and drove around looking at her old town. The next day we moved on to San Francisco, where we had lunch at Fisherman's Wharf and got to Carmel in late afternoon.

We had a great visit with Carol; a masters level Registered Nurse who works for a health service provider in Monterey County. Unfortunately, her husband Randy was in Europe attending a conference, he is a well known Psychologist. Carol, movie star beautiful herself, has two gorgeous daughters. The oldest one is the kind of young woman I didn't think they made anymore, married she loves domestic things, works with material and sews and stitches all sorts of things. She has also gotten an advanced degree in art, teaches at a college, has a baby and still finds time to do handy work and is the most pleasant personality ever. The younger one is the sweetest girl, everyone that knows her agrees. She is charming and considerate to a fault. We always stay at a hotel where she used to work, but she gave it up to pursue college. When I came to check in, I was known as Katie's uncle and women behind the desk wanted to know how she was doing and told me to have her please contact them; they miss her.

Claudia also has a cousin, Ken, who with his wife Dot, lives in Salinas, California and we spent a day with them. He is a survivor of the WWII Pacific Ocean naval battles. He served aboard the USS Salt Lake City and was in every major exchange of that Pacific war, except when they were repairing his ship. The ship was nearly sunk two times and they endured numerous causalities. He is in his eighties now and recently gave up driving; everyone was worried about the impact that might have on him. When we were out of ear-shot of the women he scoffed, "After surviving the war — a little thing like a driver's license…." He made a "puff" sound and a slight outward movement with his right hand, indicating it was trivial. He continued, "Most of us — didn't know if we'd make it." He paused, lifted his head and his eyes rolled slightly upward as he continued, "Couple of buddies—couldn't hardly find enough of 'em to bury—couple feet, an arm, burnt skull…." He went silent; we both just stood there for a few seconds, then the girls announced they were ready to go to lunch. We often went to the home of the author John Steinbeck that has been converted to a restaurant where Dot has worked as a volunteer. The Steinbeck house is a non-profit, volunteer organization dedicated to the preservation of the author's boyhood home. As always, the four of us had a wonderful time. Dot is the real cheerleader type and keeps the ball rolling wherever she is; she looks after Ken and a dozen others in her family with energy to spare, or so it would seem.

We left California via Yosemite National Park where we stayed in the world famous Ahwahnee Lodge, it's a grand place. We had a bellman help us and he told us he had been working there for 30 years. He started as a college student looking for a summer job and has been there ever since as he said looking out at the mountains, "What a great surrounding to work in." It is pretty hard to argue with that.

The next day we drove to Las Vegas intending to stay two days and wound up spending five. We then proceeded home via Flagstaff, Arizona and Santa Fe, New Mexico; but that is a whole new story....

Botanical garden in Victoria Canada

Site of the winter games 2010

I wanted to see the glaciers

Lightning Source UK Ltd.
Milton Keynes UK
UKIC01n1511181114
241762UK00012B/67

*9 7 8 1 4 4 9 0 1 8 8 2 5 *